BLACKSTONE
Griddle Bible

From Basics to Brilliance - Recipes, Maintenance, and Pro Techniques for the Ultimate Griddling Experience. Master the Best Cuts and Types of Meat for Blackstone

Rob T. Burns

TABLE OF CONTENTS

INTRODUCTION

Welcome to the sizzling world of griddling, where culinary artistry meets outdoor adventure. In the "Blackstone Griddle Bible," we embark on a journey that transcends the ordinary and opens up a realm of possibilities in the world of outdoor cooking. This is not just a cookbook; it's a comprehensive guide to grilling mastery, with a particular focus on the versatile and beloved Blackstone griddle.

Griddling isn't just a cooking technique; it's a way of life, a passion that ignites the senses and transforms meals into memorable experiences. It's about the tantalizing aroma of food sizzling on a hot griddle, the melodious sound of ingredients sputtering, and the joy of creating dishes that make taste buds dance with delight.

Why the Blackstone griddle, you might wonder? The answer is simple: it's the ultimate tool for unleashing your creativity in the kitchen. Whether you're a seasoned griddling pro or a newcomer to this exciting world, the "Blackstone Griddle Bible" has something to offer you. It's a culinary adventure that's suitable for different levels of competence, from the novice to the seasoned grill master.

Your journey begins with a heartfelt dedication to the family, a reminder that the essence of griddling extends far beyond the food on the plate. It's about creating moments, bonding with loved ones, and celebrating the joy of togetherness. It's a testament to the belief that some of life's most cherished memories are made around the grill.

This book is divided into chapters that cater to every aspect of griddling. We'll start with the basics, helping you choose the right Blackstone griddle that suits your needs and preferences. From the size and features to the critical decision of cast iron or stainless steel, we've got you covered.

As any griddling enthusiast will tell you, caring for your griddle is paramount. We'll delve into the art of cleaning and seasoning, ensuring that your griddle stays in pristine condition, ready to serve up delectable dishes. Proper maintenance and storage tips will keep your griddle in peak performance for a lifetime of culinary adventures.

Our exploration doesn't stop at the griddle itself; it extends to the essential equipment that enhances your griddling experience. We'll introduce you to an array of tools, each with its unique purpose, ensuring that you're well-equipped for any griddling challenge.

Griddle cooking styles and techniques are at the heart of this journey. From frying to wood pellet techniques, we'll explore both easy and advanced methods, equipping you with the skills to tackle any recipe that comes your way.

For those just starting, we've provided more information to kickstart your griddling adventure. You'll find a list of the best cuts and types of meat that are perfectly suited for the Blackstone griddle. Our grill temperature guide ensures that your meats are cooked to perfection, with internal temperature recommendations for each type.

The "Blackstone Griddle Bible" is not just about technique; it's also about the finer nuances of griddling. Our tips and tricks section unveils the secrets of the best sauces, spices, and seasonings, adding an extra layer of flavor to your creations. We're also committed to the environment, and our eco-friendly advice promotes sustainability in outdoor cooking.

The heart of this book lies in its recipes. From indulgent breakfasts to Tex-Mex delights, juicy burgers to succulent fish, hearty sandwiches to griddled pizzas, and even delectable desserts, we've curated a collection that's sure to tantalize your taste buds. With each recipe, we'll guide you through the ingredients, instructions, cook times, and even provide nutritional information, ensuring that your meals are not only delicious but also mindful of your dietary choices.

We'll wrap up with a comprehensive index, making it easy to find the information you need, and a set of frequently asked questions to address common queries and concerns.

So, are you ready to embark on a griddling adventure like no other? The "Blackstone Griddle Bible" is your passport to a world of flavors, techniques, and outdoor culinary joy. Let's fire up the griddle, ignite our passion for griddling, and turn every backyard BBQ into a gourmet feast. Together, we'll make you the grill master of your neighborhood, and your culinary horizons will know no bounds.

DEDICATION TO FAMILY

In the sizzle of a griddle's hot surface and the aroma of seasoned meats wafting through the air, there lies a timeless tradition that transcends the mere act of cooking. It's a connection to family, a bond forged through generations, where recipes are treasured heirlooms, and the grill becomes a sacred gathering place.

Within the pages of the "Blackstone Griddle Bible," we embark on a culinary journey rooted in the warmth of family. This dedication serves as a reminder of the love, laughter, and shared meals that define our most cherished moments. It's a tribute to those who have passed down their griddling wisdom, seasoning our lives with flavorful memories.

As you delve into the world of outdoor griddling, the importance of family will become evident. It's the grandparent who imparted their secret marinade recipe, the parent who shared their tips on perfect grill marks, and the sibling with whom you've engaged in friendly griddle cook-offs. This book is a tribute to the generations before us and a gift to those who will follow, as we embrace the art of griddling as a family legacy.

The sizzle and flip of ingredients on the Blackstone griddle are not just culinary acts but an expression of love and togetherness. This dedication stands as a testament to the power of shared meals, laughter around the griddle, and the enduring connections formed in the process. As you embark on your griddling adventures with this book as your guide, may you carry the spirit of family with you, creating new traditions and lasting memories with each delectable dish.

CHAPTER 1:
INTRODUCTION TO THE BLACKSTONE GRIDDLE BIBLE

In the world of culinary exploration, there exists a distinct allure in griddling—an art that transcends mere cooking. The "Blackstone Griddle Bible" delves into this captivating realm, where the sizzle of food meeting the griddle's surface is a symphony, and the aroma of ingredients meeting heat is poetry.

Within the pages of this book, you'll embark on a journey intertwined with my profound passion for griddling. The Blackstone griddle, in particular, holds a special place in my heart. It's not merely a piece of kitchen equipment; it's a conduit to a culinary adventure that ignites the senses and stirs the soul.

The love affair with griddling was kindled during early mornings and lazy weekends, with the promise of delectable creations that only the griddle could deliver. The Blackstone griddle, with its ample cooking space and versatility, became a canvas for my creativity, an instrument for my gastronomic symphonies.

This book is an embodiment of my devotion to the griddle, a passion that started with the simplest of pleasures—perfectly crisped bacon at dawn, the magic of pancake flips, and the unmatched sear of a well-seasoned steak. It's a journey that led to the creation of unforgettable meals shared with family and friends, each bite a testament to the joy of griddling.

As we venture together through the "Blackstone Griddle Bible," my aim is to kindle that same passion within you. Whether you're a seasoned griddle enthusiast or a novice taking your first steps into this world of flavors, this book invites you to embrace the griddle as a companion on your culinary journey. Together, we will unlock the secrets of grilling mastery, elevating your backyard barbecues to gourmet feasts and helping you claim the title of the neighborhood's grill master.

So, let us embark on this culinary voyage, and may the sizzle of your ingredients on the griddle kindle the same passion and excitement that has fueled my love for griddling. The adventure begins now.

- **The Grilling Experience of the author**

To truly understand the essence of griddling and the journey that led to the creation of the "Blackstone Griddle Bible," it's important to delve into the grilling experience of the author. Every griddler has a unique story, and here's mine.

My fascination with grilling began as a humble pursuit, one that carried me from the ordinary to the extraordinary. It was the irresistible allure of food meeting open flames, the tantalizing aroma of sizzling ingredients, and the promise of culinary artistry that captivated me. As I explored this newfound passion, I stumbled upon the Blackstone griddle, a versatile piece of cooking equipment that transformed the way I approached outdoor cooking.

The grilling experience I've gained over the years has been a voyage of discovery. It's been marked by countless mornings when the sun bathed my backyard, and the Blackstone griddle stood ready to bring my culinary visions to life. With each use, I honed my skills, learning the perfect techniques for creating dishes that not only delighted the taste buds but also engaged all the senses.

The Blackstone griddle, with its spacious cooking surface, became my canvas, and the sizzle of ingredients meeting the hot metal was my medium. From perfectly cooked breakfasts, featuring golden pancakes and crispy bacon, to sumptuous dinners, such as juicy steaks and delectable stir-fries, the griddle allowed me to explore a wide range of culinary creations.

But the grilling experience goes beyond the food. It's about the shared moments, the laughter, and the joy of gathering around the griddle with family and friends. It's about mastering the art of temperature control, seasoning, and flipping techniques to create dishes that consistently impress and satisfy.

In the "Blackstone Griddle Bible," I aim to bring you the knowledge and insights I've gained through years of passionate griddling. It's a chance to share the thrill of my grilling journey, from the first sizzle to the creation of mouthwatering feasts that have become the highlight of countless gatherings. Whether you're a seasoned griddler or a novice eager to explore the world of griddling, this book is designed to guide you on your own grilling adventure, helping you discover the joy, satisfaction, and creativity that griddling can offer.

As you dive into the pages of this book, may you be inspired by the experiences and flavors that have shaped my griddling journey. Let the sizzle of the griddle, the scent of well-seasoned dishes, and the shared moments around the table become a part of your own culinary narrative. The journey begins now.

- ### Versatility for All Levels of Competence

The beauty of the griddling experience, particularly with a versatile tool like the Blackstone griddle, lies in its accessibility to enthusiasts of all levels of competence. Whether you're a seasoned grill master or someone who's just begun to explore the world of outdoor cooking, the Blackstone griddle opens its arms wide to welcome you.

For Beginners:

For those who are just starting their griddling journey, the Blackstone griddle offers a gentle initiation. Its straightforward design and user-friendly features make it the perfect choice for novices. Even if you're not an experienced cook, you can quickly grasp the basics of griddling. The griddle's large cooking surface is forgiving, allowing you to experiment with various dishes without the fear of overcrowding.

Griddling on the Blackstone is an excellent introduction to outdoor cooking. From classic breakfast items like pancakes and eggs to simple burgers and hot dogs, the griddle's even heat distribution and precise temperature control make it easy to achieve delectable results. You'll discover that griddling is not just about the final dish; it's about the journey of sizzling, flipping, and the joy of seeing ingredients transform.

For Intermediate Grillers:

If you've already dabbled in griddling and have some experience under your belt, the Blackstone griddle is your canvas for culinary growth. You can explore a wide array of cooking techniques and start experimenting with more complex recipes. The griddle's size and heat management capabilities provide a platform to refine your skills and develop a deeper understanding of temperature control, seasoning, and flavor combinations.

The Blackstone griddle is your partner in elevating your cooking to the next level. You can venture into stir-fries, fajitas, and griddled seafood dishes that require precision and finesse. You'll appreciate the versatility of the griddle as you tackle more intricate recipes, and with each new creation, your competence as a griddler will grow.

For Advanced Grill Masters:

For seasoned grill masters, the Blackstone griddle becomes a stage for showcasing your expertise and pushing the boundaries of what's possible. The griddle's immense space and ability to maintain high temperatures make it a perfect choice for hosting larger gatherings and preparing a wide variety of dishes simultaneously.

Advanced griddlers can explore the realms of multi-course griddle dinners, from appetizers and main courses to delectable desserts. The griddle's versatility, combined with your experience, allows you to impress your guests with culinary spectacles that leave a lasting impression.

In the "Blackstone Griddle Bible," we cater to all levels of competence. Whether you're a beginner looking to start your griddling journey or an advanced griddler seeking to expand your horizons, you'll find inspiration, guidance, and recipes that align with your skill level. The Blackstone griddle offers something for everyone, and together, we'll embark on a flavorful adventure that caters to your expertise, whether budding or seasoned.

CHAPTER 2:
CHOOSING THE RIGHT BLACKSTONE GRIDDLE

When it comes to selecting the perfect Blackstone griddle for your outdoor cooking adventures, several factors come into play. The right griddle should cater to your specific needs, space availability, and cooking preferences. In this section, we'll explore the key considerations to help you make an informed choice.

1. Size Matters:

One of the fundamental decisions when choosing a Blackstone griddle is its size. Griddles come in various dimensions, typically measured in square inches of cooking surface. Your choice of size depends on how much cooking space you require and the available space in your outdoor cooking area. Here are the primary size options:

- **1seven-Inch Tabletop Griddle:** Perfect for solo cooks, couples, or those with limited outdoor space.

- **2two-Inch Griddle:** A popular choice for small families or gatherings.

- **2eight-Inch Griddle:** Ideal for mid-sized families and gatherings.

- **3six-Inch Griddle:** The go-to option for larger families or hosting bigger parties.

Consider your typical cooking needs and the number of people you'll be serving. It's essential to strike a balance between having enough cooking space and not overcommitting to a griddle that's larger than necessary.

2. Features that Matter:

Blackstone griddles come with a range of features that enhance your cooking experience. Here are some key features to consider:

- **Foldable Legs or Wheels:** Griddles with foldable legs or wheels offer portability and convenience. You can easily move your griddle around and store it when not in use.

- **Hood or Lid:** Some models come with a hood or lid, which is great for trapping heat and smoke, creating an oven-like environment for baking and roasting.

- **Built-in Grease Management:** Look for models with effective grease management systems that make cleanup a breeze.

- **Burners and Heat Zones:** Griddles may have one or more burners, each with its heat control. Multiple heat zones allow you to cook different foods at varying temperatures simultaneously.

- **Ignition System:** Some griddles have a convenient push-button ignition system, making startup quick and hassle-free.

- **Side Shelves and Hooks:** These are handy for keeping cooking utensils, spices, and accessories within arm's reach.

3. Choosing the Right Brand:

Blackstone has established itself as a trusted brand in the world of griddling, known for its quality and innovation. When choosing a Blackstone griddle, you can have confidence in the brand's reputation for durability and performance. You may also find variations in the product lines, such as the Blackstone Pro Series or Adventure Ready models, each catering to different needs and preferences.

It's always a good idea to read product reviews and do some research on the specific model you're interested in to ensure it meets your expectations and requirements.

Ultimately, selecting the right Blackstone griddle comes down to your individual circumstances and preferences. Consider the size, features, and brand that align with your cooking goals and the space available in your outdoor cooking area. With the right griddle in your arsenal, you'll be well on your way to unlocking the secrets of grilling mastery.

- ### Cast-Iron vs. Stainless Steel

When it comes to choosing the material for your Blackstone griddle, you'll likely encounter two primary options: cast-iron and stainless steel. Each material has its own set of advantages and considerations. Let's explore the differences between cast-iron and stainless steel griddles to help you make an informed decision.

Cast-Iron Griddles:

1. **Heat Retention:** Cast-iron is renowned for its exceptional heat retention. It heats evenly and holds the heat well, making it ideal for even cooking and maintaining a consistent temperature across the cooking surface.

2. **Seasoning:** Cast-iron griddles require seasoning to develop a natural non-stick surface. This involves applying a layer of oil or grease and heating it to create a protective coating. Over time, this seasoning enhances the griddle's non-stick properties and imparts a unique flavor to your food.

3. **Durability:** Cast-iron griddles are durable and long-lasting. With proper care, they can last for generations and even become family heirlooms.

4. **Flavor Enhancement:** The porous nature of cast-iron can absorb and release flavors over time, adding a subtle depth of flavor to your dishes.

5. **Maintenance:** While cast-iron griddles are relatively low-maintenance, they require proper cleaning and occasional re-seasoning to prevent rust and maintain their non-stick properties.

Stainless Steel Griddles:

1. **Durability:** Stainless steel griddles are incredibly durable and resistant to rust, corrosion, and staining. They can withstand exposure to the elements and are easy to clean.

2. **Cleanliness:** Stainless steel is non-porous, which means it won't absorb flavors or odors from previous meals. This makes it a great choice for those who want a neutral cooking surface.

3. **Ease of Cleaning:** Stainless steel griddles are typically easier to clean and require less maintenance than cast-iron griddles. They can often be cleaned with a simple wipe-down.

4. **Heat Distribution:** While stainless steel griddles provide even heat distribution, they may not retain heat as effectively as cast-iron, which can be a consideration for certain cooking techniques.

5. **No Seasoning Required:** Unlike cast-iron, stainless steel griddles do not require seasoning. They have a natural non-stick surface that doesn't require additional treatment.

Choosing Between Cast-Iron and Stainless Steel:

The choice between cast-iron and stainless steel ultimately depends on your cooking style, preferences, and maintenance considerations. Here are some factors to consider:

• If you appreciate the flavor enhancement and are willing to invest in maintenance, cast-iron is an excellent choice.

• If you prefer easy maintenance and a neutral cooking surface, stainless steel may be the better option.

• Durability and longevity are important, and both materials excel in this regard.

In the end, the "best" choice depends on your individual needs and cooking style. Whichever material you choose, the Blackstone griddle experience will open the door to a world of outdoor cooking possibilities.

CHAPTER 3:
CARING FOR YOUR GRIDDLE

Proper care and maintenance of your Blackstone griddle are essential to ensure its longevity and cooking performance. In this section, we'll explore the important practices of cleaning and seasoning your griddle.

Cleaning Your Griddle:

1. **After Each Use:**

• Scrape off any food debris and grease using a griddle scraper or spatula while the griddle is still hot.

• Wipe the surface with a damp cloth or paper towels to remove remaining residue. Be cautious of steam and hot surfaces.

2. **Deep Cleaning:**

• For more thorough cleaning, especially when dealing with stubborn grease or buildup, you can use a mixture of water and a mild dishwashing soap. Apply the soapy water to the griddle's surface and scrub gently with a griddle cleaning brush or scouring pad.

• Rinse thoroughly with water and wipe dry. Ensure there is no soap residue left on the surface.

3. **Removing Rust:** If you notice any rust spots on your griddle, use a scrubber or steel wool to gently remove the rust. Afterward, wash and re-season the affected area.

4. **Grease Tray and Drip Pan:** Regularly empty and clean the grease tray and drip pan to prevent excess grease buildup and maintain proper drainage.

Seasoning Your Griddle:

Seasoning is the process of applying a layer of oil to your griddle to protect it from rust and create a natural non-stick surface. Here's how to season your Blackstone griddle:

1. **Clean the Griddle:** Start with a clean, dry griddle. Ensure all food residue and moisture are removed.

2. **Heat the Griddle:** Turn on your griddle and heat it to a medium-high temperature (around 350-375°F or 17five-190°C). Heating the griddle opens the pores of the metal, allowing the oil to penetrate.

3. **Apply Oil:** Use a high smoke-point oil like vegetable oil, canola oil, or flaxseed oil. Apply a thin, even layer of oil to the griddle's surface using a cloth or paper towel. Be careful not to use too much oil, as it can create a sticky residue.

4. **Spread the Oil:** Use a clean cloth or paper towel to spread the oil across the griddle's surface, including the cooking area and the sides.

5. **Repeat the Process:** You may need to repeat the oil application and heating process two-four times to build up a good seasoning layer. This initial seasoning is essential for the griddle's non-stick properties and rust resistance.

6. **Cool Down:** Allow the griddle to cool down completely. The seasoning process is complete, and your griddle is ready for future use.

Maintaining the Seasoning:

To maintain the seasoning on your griddle, follow these practices:

-   After each use, clean your griddle as mentioned above.

-   After cleaning, apply a thin layer of oil to the surface while it's still warm (but not hot). This helps to reinforce the seasoning.

-   Store your griddle in a dry place to prevent moisture and humidity from affecting the seasoning.

By regularly cleaning and seasoning your Blackstone griddle, you'll not only protect it from rust but also ensure a non-stick surface that enhances your cooking experience. This care and attention will contribute to the longevity of your griddle, allowing it to serve you for many enjoyable griddling adventures.

- **Proper Maintenance**

Maintaining your Blackstone griddle is vital to keep it in excellent condition and extend its lifespan. Proper maintenance ensures that your griddle continues to perform at its best and provides you with many years of delicious outdoor cooking. Here are essential maintenance tips to follow:

1. **Regular Cleaning:**

- As mentioned in the previous section, clean your griddle after each use. Remove food residue and grease to prevent the buildup of carbon deposits, which can affect the cooking surface and lead to uneven heat distribution.

- Deep clean the griddle as needed, especially if there's stubborn residue. Use mild dishwashing soap, warm water, and a griddle cleaning brush or scouring pad. Rinse thoroughly and dry.

2. **Grease Management:**

- Empty the grease tray and drip pan regularly to prevent overflows and maintain proper drainage. Dispose of the collected grease properly.

- Inspect the grease management system for any clogs or blockages. Ensure that grease can flow freely.

3. **Check for Rust:**

- Periodically inspect your griddle for any signs of rust. If you spot rust, gently remove it using a scrubber or steel wool. Afterward, re-season the affected area to prevent further rusting.

4. **Burner Maintenance:**

- Inspect the burners and ignition system for any blockages, corrosion, or damage. Clean the burners if necessary to ensure they operate efficiently.

5. **Protective Cover:**

- When not in use, cover your griddle with a weather-resistant protective cover. This protects it from the elements, including rain, snow, and UV exposure, which can lead to premature wear and rust.

6. **Inspect Hoses and Connectors:**

- If your griddle is a gas model, check the gas hoses and connectors for any signs of wear, damage, or leaks. Ensure they are in good condition and replace them if needed.

7. **Store Properly:**

- Store your griddle in a dry, cool, and well-ventilated area. Avoid storing it in a damp or humid environment, as this can lead to rust and damage.

8. **Regular Seasoning:**

- Maintain the seasoning of your griddle by re-seasoning it as needed, as described in the previous section. Frequent use may require more frequent seasoning.

9. **Periodic Inspection:**

- Occasionally inspect all parts of your griddle, including the frame, legs, and shelves, for any signs of wear, rust, or damage. Replace or repair any worn or damaged components promptly.

10. **User Manual Reference:**

- Always consult your griddle's user manual for manufacturer-specific maintenance instructions and recommendations.

Proper maintenance not only preserves the functionality and appearance of your Blackstone griddle but also contributes to your cooking experience. By following these maintenance guidelines and staying attentive to the condition of your griddle, you'll ensure that it remains a reliable and enjoyable tool for your outdoor cooking adventures.

- **Storage Tips**

Proper storage of your Blackstone griddle is crucial to protect it from the elements and maintain its performance over time. Whether you're storing it for the winter or just between uses, follow these storage tips to keep your griddle in excellent condition:

1. **Clean Thoroughly:**

- Before storing your griddle, make sure it's completely clean. Follow the cleaning and seasoning steps as outlined in previous sections to remove any food residue and prevent rust.

2. **Ensure Dryness:**

- Ensure that your griddle is completely dry before storing it. Moisture can lead to rust and corrosion over time.

3. **Apply a Protective Cover:**

- Invest in a weather-resistant, UV-resistant, and breathable cover designed for your specific griddle model. Cover your griddle completely to protect it from rain, snow, and sun exposure.

4. **Securely Store the Grease Tray:**

- If your griddle has a removable grease tray, make sure it's empty and clean. Store it separately in a dry place to prevent grease buildup and potential odors.

5. **Store in a Dry Location:**

- Choose a storage location that is dry and well-ventilated. Avoid storing your griddle in damp or humid environments, such as basements or areas prone to moisture, as this can lead to rust and damage.

6. **Elevate if Possible:**

- If your storage area allows, elevate the griddle off the ground. Placing it on a platform, wooden pallet, or a set of bricks can help prevent moisture and pests from reaching the griddle.

7. **Check the Grease Management System:**

• Ensure that the grease management system is clean and free of clogs before storage. This helps prevent blockages and ensures proper drainage when you use the griddle again.

8. **Keep Accessories Together:**

• Store griddle accessories, such as spatulas, brushes, and grill tools, together with your griddle or in a designated storage container.

9. **Secure Loose Parts:**

• If your griddle has removable parts, like side shelves or wind guards, remove and store them in a secure and dry location to prevent damage or rust.

10. **Periodic Inspection:**

• While your griddle is in storage, periodically check on it to ensure it remains clean, dry, and in good condition. This practice can help you address any issues promptly.

11. **Maintain Seasoning:**

• Periodically re-season your griddle, even during storage, to maintain its non-stick surface and rust resistance.

By following these storage tips, you can ensure that your Blackstone griddle remains in top-notch condition and ready for use whenever you decide to fire it up for your next outdoor cooking adventure. Proper storage preserves your investment and prolongs the lifespan of your griddle.

CHAPTER 4:
ESSENTIAL EQUIPMENT

To become a true griddle master, you'll need the right tools at your disposal. The Blackstone griddle is a versatile cooking surface, and with the proper equipment, you can unlock its full potential. Here's an in-depth look at the essential tools for griddling:

1. **Griddle Scraper:** A griddle scraper is your best friend for cleaning the griddle. This essential tool features a sturdy, flat blade designed to effortlessly remove food residue and grease buildup. As you griddle, you'll find that a quick scrape between batches ensures a clean and sanitary cooking surface. Look for scrapers with long handles to keep your hands safely away from the heat.

2. **Spatulas:** Invest in a set of high-quality spatulas with different shapes and sizes. These versatile tools are crucial for flipping and turning food on the griddle. A long, thin spatula is perfect for flipping delicate items like pancakes and eggs, while a wide, sturdy spatula is ideal for handling burgers, steaks, and larger items. The right spatula can make the difference between a perfectly executed flip and a potential mishap.

3. **Tongs:** Tongs are indispensable tools for griddling. These versatile utensils are perfect for flipping delicate items like shrimp or asparagus and for moving food around the griddle with precision. Look for tongs with a comfortable grip and a locking mechanism for easy storage.

4. **Griddle Cleaning Brush:** A griddle cleaning brush with heat-resistant bristles is an excellent addition to your griddle toolkit. This tool is perfect for deep cleaning and helps you remove stubborn residue and grease buildup without scratching the griddle surface. An effective cleaning brush is a time-saver and ensures that your griddle remains in top condition.

5. **Oil Dispenser:** An oil dispenser is a handy addition to your griddle setup. It allows you to apply oil to the griddle's surface evenly, which is particularly useful for seasoning the griddle

before and after cooking. Look for a dispenser with a controlled pouring spout to prevent over-application of oil, which can lead to flare-ups.

6. **Meat Thermometer:** A meat thermometer is an indispensable tool for grilling meats to perfection. Whether you're cooking steaks, burgers, or poultry, a meat thermometer ensures that your food is cooked to your desired level of doneness. This tool eliminates the guesswork and guarantees consistently delicious results.

7. **Basting Cover:** A basting cover, also known as a dome, is a versatile accessory for your griddle. It can be used to trap heat and steam, allowing you to melt cheese, finish cooking, or create a convection oven effect for baking and roasting on the griddle. A basting cover is particularly useful for cooking foods that benefit from even heat distribution and moisture retention.

8. **Heat-Resistant Gloves:** Safety is paramount when griddling, and heat-resistant gloves are essential for your protection. These gloves are designed to withstand high temperatures and protect your hands from burns and discomfort. Heat-resistant gloves allow you to handle hot griddle accessories, move hot pans, and make adjustments to your griddle setup without worry.

9. **Measuring** Cupful **and Spoons:** Griddling often involves following recipes, and accurate measurements are vital for success. Having a set of measuring cupful and spoons on hand ensures that you can add the right amount of ingredients, whether it's for marinades, sauces, or seasoning blends. Accurate measurements are the key to achieving the perfect balance of flavors.

10. **Wire Cooling Rack:** A wire cooling rack is a practical addition to your griddling toolkit. It's particularly useful for resting cooked food, allowing excess oil or moisture to drip away. This helps keep fried and greasy items crispy while preventing them from becoming soggy. Wire cooling racks are excellent for holding batches of fried foods and are especially handy for achieving the ideal texture.

11. **Storage Containers:** Griddling often involves prepping ingredients, marinating meats, and storing leftovers. Having a selection of airtight containers for ingredients and cooked food is essential for keeping your griddling area organized and ensuring that ingredients remain

fresh. These containers come in various sizes, making them suitable for everything from storing chopped vegetables to marinating meats or keeping leftovers in the refrigerator.

12. **Paper Towels and Cloth Towels:** Keep a ready supply of paper towels and cloth towels within arm's reach. These versatile tools are essential for cleaning, wiping down surfaces, and handling hot utensils. Paper towels are perfect for quick cleanups and blotting excess oil, while cloth towels can be used to protect your hands when handling hot utensils and to maintain a tidy cooking area.

13. **Griddle Cover:** A weather-resistant griddle cover is a valuable accessory to protect your investment when your griddle is not in use. The cover shields your griddle from the elements, including rain, snow, and UV exposure, which can lead to premature wear and rust. A properly fitted cover keeps your griddle clean and ready for your next cooking adventure.

14. **Table or Shelf:** Having a stable surface near your griddle is invaluable for prepping ingredients, storing utensils, and maintaining an organized cooking area. A sturdy table or shelf provides a convenient location for your propane tank, utensils, seasonings, and more. It ensures that everything you need is within arm's reach, streamlining your griddling experience.

With these essential tools for griddling at your disposal, you'll be well-prepared to tackle a wide range of recipes and cooking techniques on your Blackstone griddle. These tools make the griddling experience efficient, safe, and enjoyable, allowing you to create mouthwatering dishes and become a true griddle master.

- **Techniques for Using Each Tool**

To master the art of griddling and make the most of your essential griddle tools, you'll want to understand the techniques for using each one effectively. Here's an in-depth look at techniques for using these tools:

1. **Griddle Scraper:**

- **Technique:** Hold the griddle scraper at a slight angle to the griddle surface and apply downward pressure. Scrape any food residue or grease in a sweeping motion. Repeat as needed, using short strokes.

- **Tip:** Use a firm but controlled motion to avoid damaging the griddle surface. Be sure to scrape while the griddle is still hot, which makes it easier to remove residue. The griddle scraper is your trusty companion for maintaining a clean cooking surface, ensuring your food doesn't stick and maintaining a sanitary environment.

2. **Spatulas:**

- **Technique:** When flipping food, slide the spatula beneath the item you're cooking, gently lift it, and flip it over. Use a combination of a smooth, fluid wrist motion and a gentle lift for best results.

- **Tip:** Different spatulas are designed for various tasks. Use a thin, long spatula for delicate items like eggs and pancakes, while a wider spatula is ideal for handling heartier items like burgers and steaks. Mastering the art of spatula work ensures that your food remains intact and perfectly cooked.

3. **Tongs:**

- **Technique:** When using tongs, grip the food firmly but not too tightly. Flip, turn, or move food on the griddle with a smooth and precise motion, maintaining control over the food.

- **Tip:** Tongs are versatile and useful for various griddling tasks, from flipping burgers to arranging vegetables. Practice using them gently to avoid crushing delicate items. Tongs give you the dexterity needed to handle food with precision.

4. **Griddle Cleaning Brush:**

- **Technique:** Apply moderate pressure while brushing the griddle's surface in a back-and-forth motion. Focus on areas with stubborn residue or grease buildup. Rinse the brush and repeat as needed.

- **Tip:** Use a griddle cleaning brush when the griddle is still warm to loosen residue effectively. Avoid using excessive force to prevent scratching the griddle. The griddle cleaning brush ensures your cooking surface is pristine and ready for the next culinary masterpiece.

5. **Oil Dispenser:**

• **Technique:** Hold the oil dispenser upright and apply a slow, even stream of oil to the griddle's surface. Move your hand in a controlled manner to distribute the oil evenly.

• **Tip:** Use a high smoke-point oil like vegetable or canola oil. Applying oil in a circular or zigzag pattern helps ensure even coverage. The oil dispenser allows you to effortlessly season the griddle and prevent sticking while cooking.

6. **Meat Thermometer:**

• **Technique:** Insert the meat thermometer into the thickest part of the meat, avoiding bones or fat. Ensure that the thermometer's tip is at the center of the meat to obtain an accurate temperature reading.

• **Tip:** For precise doneness, consult recommended internal temperature guidelines for different types of meat and desired levels of doneness. A meat thermometer is your guide to perfectly cooked meats every time.

7. **Basting Cover:**

• **Technique:** Place the basting cover over the food you're cooking to trap heat and steam. This method helps melt cheese, finish cooking, or create a convection oven effect for baking and roasting.

• **Tip:** When using a basting cover, make sure it fits over your food and griddle area completely for even cooking and heat retention. The basting cover enhances your cooking options and allows for a variety of techniques.

8. **Heat-Resistant Gloves:**

• **Technique:** Wear heat-resistant gloves when handling hot griddle accessories, making adjustments to your griddle setup, or moving hot pans. Ensure the gloves are well-fitted to provide maximum protection.

• **Tip:** Choose gloves that offer a secure grip to prevent accidents while handling hot items on the griddle. Heat-resistant gloves are your safety net for hassle-free griddling.

9. **Measuring** Cupful **and Spoons:**

- **Technique:** Use measuring cupful and spoons to accurately measure ingredients, ensuring precise quantities for your recipes. Level off dry ingredients like flour or sugar for accurate measurements.

- **Tip:** Invest in a set of measuring cupful and spoons made of durable, easy-to-clean materials. Accurate measurements are the foundation of culinary success.

10. **Wire Cooling Rack:**

- **Technique:** Place the wire cooling rack on a clean surface and transfer cooked food to it for resting. Ensure that excess oil or moisture drips away, preserving the food's texture and preventing sogginess.

- **Tip:** Wire cooling racks are ideal for items like fried chicken, tempura, and other crispy foods. They help maintain the desired level of crispiness, ensuring that your creations stay perfect until they reach the plate.

11. **Storage Containers:**

- **Technique:** Use airtight storage containers to store ingredients, marinate meats, and keep leftovers fresh. Make sure to seal the containers tightly to prevent air and moisture from entering.

- **Tip:** Label containers with the contents and date to keep track of your ingredients and leftovers. Storage containers are your organization allies, keeping your kitchen efficient and well-prepared.

12. **Paper Towels and Cloth Towels:**

- **Technique:** Use paper towels for quick cleanups, blotting excess oil, and disposing of greasy items. Cloth towels are excellent for protecting your hands when handling hot utensils and maintaining a tidy cooking area.

- **Tip:** Keep paper towels and cloth towels in a convenient location for easy access during griddling. These humble tools are your partners in keeping your workspace neat and clean.

By mastering these techniques for using each griddle tool effectively, you'll enhance your griddling skills and make your outdoor cooking experience smoother and more enjoyable. These skills, combined with the right tools, will help you achieve griddling success and create delectable dishes that impress family and friends.

CHAPTER 5:
GRIDDLE COOKING STYLES AND TECHNIQUES

- **Frying on the Griddle**

Frying on the griddle is a versatile and beloved cooking style that allows you to achieve crispy, golden-brown perfection in a wide range of dishes. Whether you're frying up classic favorites or exploring new horizons, the Blackstone griddle is your ideal companion. Here's a closer look at frying on the griddle, including essential techniques and tips:

Frying Basics:

1. **Temperature Control:** One of the key elements of successful frying is maintaining the right cooking temperature. Most griddles provide even and consistent heat, making it easier to achieve the perfect fry. Adjust the griddle's heat settings based on the specific food you're frying.

2. **Oil Selection:** Choose an oil with a high smoke point for frying, such as vegetable oil, peanut oil, or canola oil. The oil should be able to withstand the high temperatures required for frying without breaking down or smoking excessively.

3. **Preheating:** Preheat the griddle to the desired temperature before adding the oil. Proper preheating ensures that the food starts cooking immediately and forms a crispy crust.

4. **Breading and Coating:** To achieve a crunchy exterior, many fried dishes are coated with a breading or batter. Dip the food in a wet batter (flour and liquid mixture) or apply a dry coating (such as breadcrumbs or flour) to create the desired texture.

5. **Frying Time:** Monitor the frying time carefully, as it can vary depending on the thickness of the food and the griddle temperature. Keep an eye on the color and texture of the food to determine when it's perfectly fried.

Frying Techniques:

1. **Shallow Frying:** Shallow frying involves cooking food partially submerged in oil. This technique is suitable for foods like pancakes, latkes, or shallow-fried chicken. Use enough oil to cover the bottom of the griddle.

2. **Deep Frying:** Deep frying entails fully submerging food in hot oil. While deep frying is often associated with dedicated deep fryers, you can safely deep fry on a griddle with proper oil depth. Use a deep, heavy pan on the griddle, fill it with oil, and heat it to the desired temperature.

3. **Pan-Frying:** Pan-frying is a common technique for foods like chicken cutlets and fish fillets. Use a small amount of oil, and cook the food directly on the griddle surface. Flip the food as needed to ensure even cooking and a golden crust.

Tips for Successful Frying:

1. **Use a Thermometer:** A thermometer is invaluable for maintaining the correct frying temperature. It helps you avoid undercooking or overcooking your food and ensures a perfect fry every time.

2. **Pat Dry:** Before frying, pat the food dry with paper towels to remove excess moisture. Dry food creates a crisper texture when it meets the hot oil.

3. **Avoid Crowding:** Overcrowding the griddle can lower the oil's temperature and result in uneven frying. Cook food in batches to maintain the oil's heat and achieve consistent results.

4. **Drain Excess Oil:** After frying, place the food on a wire rack or a plate lined with paper towels to allow excess oil to drain away. This step keeps your fried dishes from becoming greasy.

5. **Season Immediately:** Season your fried dishes with salt or other seasonings while they're still hot. The seasoning will adhere better and infuse the food with flavor.

6. **Safety First:** Be cautious when working with hot oil to prevent splatters and burns. Use long tongs or a slotted spoon to add and remove food from the oil.

Frying on the griddle opens up a world of possibilities, from classic French fries to crispy chicken tenders and tempura vegetables. With the right techniques and attention to detail, you can create a wide array of delicious fried dishes, impressing your guests and elevating your griddling skills.

- **Wood Pellet Techniques**

Griddling with wood pellets adds a unique and smoky flavor to your outdoor cooking experience. If you're looking to infuse your dishes with the rich aroma and taste of wood smoke, here are the essential techniques and tips for griddling with wood pellets:

Wood Pellet Basics:

1. **Select the Right Wood Pellets:** Choose wood pellets that complement the flavors of your dishes. Popular options include hickory for a strong, smoky taste, applewood for a sweeter profile, and mesquite for a robust flavor. Experiment with different types to find your favorites.

2. **Pellet Hopper and Auger System:** Many griddles designed for wood pellet grilling come equipped with a pellet hopper and auger system. This automated system feeds the pellets into the firebox as needed, maintaining a consistent temperature.

3. **Preheat the Griddle:** Start by preheating your griddle to the desired temperature, just like you would with a traditional grilling method.

4. **Adjust the Grill Settings:** Most wood pellet griddles have temperature control settings. Choose the temperature that aligns with your recipe, whether you're searing, smoking, or slow-cooking.

Wood Pellet Techniques:

1. **Direct Griddling:** For direct griddling with wood pellets, place your food directly on the griddle's surface. This technique is ideal for searing steaks, cooking burgers, and griddling vegetables with a smoky twist.

2. **Indirect Griddling:** Indirect griddling involves cooking food next to, rather than directly over, the wood pellet fire. This technique is suitable for slow-cooking or smoking dishes like ribs, brisket, and whole poultry.

3. **Searing:** To achieve a perfect sear on steaks or other cuts of meat, preheat the griddle on high heat, then sear the meat for a short period on each side. This technique locks in juices and imparts a smoky flavor.

4. **Smoking:** For a smoky infusion, use the wood pellet griddle as a smoker. Lower the temperature, place a smoker box or foil packet of soaked wood pellets on the griddle, and smoke your ingredients. This technique works well for fish, poultry, and ribs.

5. **Low and Slow:** When griddling at lower temperatures, you can slow-cook or roast meats and other dishes. Maintain a steady temperature, and be patient. This method is perfect for pulled pork, beef roasts, and more.

Tips for Successful Wood Pellet Griddling:

1. **Monitor Temperature:** Keep a close eye on the griddle's temperature to ensure consistent cooking. Adjust the settings as needed to maintain the desired level of heat.

2. **Soak Wood Pellets:** If you're using wood pellets for smoking, soak them in water before use to create more smoke and less heat. Soaked pellets release a rich, flavorful smoke that enhances your dishes.

3. **Experiment:** Wood pellet griddling offers an array of possibilities. Experiment with different wood types, temperatures, and cooking times to find the perfect combination for your favorite dishes.

4. **Maintenance:** Keep your wood pellet griddle clean and well-maintained. Regularly clean out the firebox and ash buildup to ensure optimal performance.

5. **Safety:** Remember that wood pellet griddles, like other grilling methods, involve open flames. Ensure safety by following safety guidelines and keeping a fire extinguisher nearby.

Griddling with wood pellets is a fantastic way to add depth and complexity to your outdoor cooking. By mastering these techniques and exploring the variety of wood pellet flavors, you'll elevate your griddling game and create dishes that are rich in smoky goodness.

- **Easy and Advanced Techniques**

Griddling offers a wide range of cooking techniques, suitable for both beginners and seasoned grill masters. Here, we'll explore a spectrum of techniques, from easy to advanced, to cater to all levels of griddling expertise:

Easy Techniques:

1. **Direct Cooking:** This is the simplest griddling technique. It involves cooking food directly on the griddle surface. It's perfect for items like burgers, hot dogs, and pancakes. Simply preheat the griddle and place the food directly on it for quick and straightforward cooking.

2. **Sautéing:** Sautéing on the griddle is as easy as it gets. Use a small amount of oil or butter, and cook your favorite vegetables, shrimp, or diced chicken. It's a fast and healthy way to prepare delicious dishes.

3. **Flatbreads and Quesadillas:** Making flatbreads and quesadillas on the griddle is a breeze. Spread your choice of toppings on a tortilla or flatbread, fold it in half, and cook until it's crispy and the cheese is melted.

4. **Stir-Frying:** You can stir-fry a variety of ingredients on the griddle. Heat oil, add your favorite veggies, protein, and sauces, and stir-fry for a quick and flavorful meal. It's a simple way to create a restaurant-quality stir-fry at home.

Advanced Techniques:

1. **Reverse Searing:** Reverse searing is an advanced technique for achieving a perfect crust on your steaks. Start by cooking the meat at a low temperature on the griddle, then finish with a high-heat sear. This method ensures a juicy interior and a flavorful crust.

2. **Smash Burgers:** To make a classic smash burger, you'll need to master the art of smashing. Form your burger patty, place it on the griddle, and use a spatula to smash it down. This technique creates a thin, crispy crust that's beloved by burger enthusiasts.

3. **Deglazing:** Deglazing involves adding liquid, such as wine, broth, or vinegar, to the griddle after cooking meat. It loosens the flavorful browned bits on the griddle and creates a rich, delicious sauce. This technique is perfect for enhancing the taste of your dishes.

4. **Griddle Baking:** Baking on the griddle requires precise temperature control. It's advanced because you'll need to maintain an even temperature, whether you're baking pizza, bread, or cookies. This technique lets you enjoy the flavors of the grill in your baked goods.

5. **Multi-Zone Griddling:** This technique involves creating multiple heat zones on your griddle by adjusting the burners. You can cook different foods at varying temperatures simultaneously. It's a versatile method for preparing a complete meal on a single griddle.

As you explore griddling, you can start with the easy techniques and gradually work your way up to the advanced ones. With practice, you'll become a griddle master, capable of creating a wide array of delicious dishes that will impress your family and friends.

CHAPTER 6:
MORE INFORMATION FOR START

When it comes to griddling, choosing the right cuts and types of meat can make all the difference in the outcome of your dishes. Whether you're a seasoned griddler or just starting, understanding the best cuts and meat varieties is crucial for achieving delicious results. Here's a comprehensive guide to help you make informed choices:

Beef:

1. **Ribeye Steak:** Known for its marbling and rich flavor, the ribeye steak is a favorite among griddling enthusiasts. It's best cooked to medium-rare or medium for a tender, juicy result.

2. **New York Strip:** This cut offers a balance of tenderness and flavor. It's versatile and can be cooked to your preferred doneness, from rare to well-done.

3. **Filet Mignon:** As one of the most tender cuts of beef, filet mignon is perfect for griddling. It's often cooked to medium-rare or medium to preserve its tenderness and subtle flavor.

4. **Hamburger Patties:** Ground beef is a classic choice for griddling. Form your own patties using ground beef, seasoning, and shape them to your desired thickness. Grill to your preferred level of doneness.

5. **Skirt Steak:** Skirt steak is flavorful and relatively affordable. Marinate it to enhance its taste, then grill quickly on high heat and slice against the grain for maximum tenderness.

Pork:

1. **Pork Chops:** Thick-cut pork chops are a delicious choice for griddling. Season them and cook to an internal temperature of 145°F (63°C) for a juicy and flavorful result.

2. **Pork Tenderloin:** Pork tenderloin is a lean and tender cut. Marinate it to infuse flavor and grill until the internal temperature reaches 145°F (63°C).

3. **Pork Shoulder (Pulled Pork):** Griddling isn't just for quick cooking; it's also great for low and slow preparations. Pork shoulder, when slow-cooked on the griddle, can be pulled apart for mouthwatering pulled pork sandwiches.

Poultry:

1. **Chicken Breasts:** Griddle chicken breasts for a lean and healthy option. Season them and cook to an internal temperature of 165°F (74°C).

2. **Chicken Thighs:** Chicken thighs are juicier and more forgiving than breasts. Griddle to an internal temperature of 165°F (74°C) for tender and flavorful results.

3. **Whole Chicken:** For a unique griddling experience, spatchcock a whole chicken (remove the backbone), season it, and cook it skin-side down on the griddle. This method ensures crispy skin and juicy meat.

Fish:

1. **Salmon:** Salmon is an excellent choice for griddling. The high heat of the griddle sears the skin and locks in moisture. Cook it skin-side down until it's easily flaked with a fork.

2. **Shrimp:** Shrimp cook quickly on the griddle. Season them and grill for a few minutes on each side until they turn pink and opaque.

3. **Tuna:** Tuna steaks are a favorite for griddling. Sear them on high heat for a short time to keep the interior rare or medium-rare.

4. **Scallops:** Scallops are sweet and tender when cooked on the griddle. Sear them briefly for a golden crust and a tender interior.

5. **Whitefish:** Griddle whitefish fillets for a simple and tasty meal. Season them and grill until they easily flake with a fork.

Choosing the right cuts and types of meat is the foundation of successful griddling. Whether you prefer beef, pork, poultry, or fish, understanding the characteristics of each meat variety and how to cook them to perfection is key to achieving mouthwatering results. Experiment with different cuts and types to discover your favorite griddling experiences.

- **Grill Temperature Guide**

Grilling at the correct temperature is essential for achieving the perfect level of doneness and flavor in your dishes. Here's a comprehensive grill temperature guide that covers various types of meat and recommended grill temperatures for different parts or cuts:

Beef:

1. **Steak:**

- **Rare:** Grill at 125°F (52°C) for two-three minutes per side.

- **Medium-Rare:** Grill at 135°F (57°C) for three-four minutes per side.

- **Medium:** Grill at 145°F (63°C) for four-five minutes per side.

- **Medium-Well:** Grill at 155°F (68°C) for five-six minutes per side.

- **Well-Done:** Grill at 160°F (71°C) for six-seven minutes per side.

2. **Burgers:**

- **Rare:** Grill at 120°F (49°C) for two-three minutes per side.

- **Medium-Rare:** Grill at 130°F (54°C) for three-four minutes per side.

- **Medium:** Grill at 140°F (60°C) for four-five minutes per side.

- **Medium-Well:** Grill at 150°F (66°C) for five-six minutes per side.

- **Well-Done:** Grill at 160°F (71°C) for six-seven minutes per side.

3. **Roasts:**

- **Rare:** Grill at 120-130°F (49-54°C) for 10-fifteen minutes per pound.

- **Medium-Rare:** Grill at 130-140°F (5four-60°C) for fifteen-20 minutes per pound.

- **Medium:** Grill at 140-150°F (60-66°C) for 20-Twenty Five minutes per pound.

- **Medium-Well:** Grill at 150-160°F (6six-71°C) for Twenty Five-30 minutes per pound.

- **Well-Done:** Grill at 160°F (71°C) and above for 30-3five minutes per pound.

Pork:

1. **Pork Chops:**

- **Medium-Rare:** Grill at 135°F (57°C) for three-four minutes per side.

- **Medium:** Grill at 145°F (63°C) for four-five minutes per side.

- **Medium-Well:** Grill at 150°F (66°C) for five-six minutes per side.

2. **Pork Tenderloin:**

- **Medium-Rare:** Grill at 140°F (60°C) for 20-Twenty Five minutes.

- **Medium:** Grill at 145°F (63°C) for Twenty Five-30 minutes.

- **Medium-Well:** Grill at 150°F (66°C) for 30-3five minutes.

3. **Pork Shoulder (Pulled Pork):**

- **Low and Slow:** Grill at 2Twenty Five-250°F (10seven-121°C) for six-eight hours.

Poultry:

1. **Chicken Breasts:**

- **Boneless, Skinless:** Grill at 165°F (74°C) for six-eight minutes per side.

- **Bone-In, Skin-On:** Grill at 165°F (74°C) for 20-30 minutes per side.

2. **Chicken Thighs:**

- **Boneless, Skinless:** Grill at 165°F (74°C) for four-six minutes per side.

- **Bone-In, Skin-On:** Grill at 165°F (74°C) for fifteen-20 minutes per side.

3. **Whole Chicken:**

- **Spatchcocked:** Grill at 350-375°F (17seven-191°C) for 50-7five minutes.

Fish:

1. **Salmon:**

• **Medium-Rare:** Grill at 1Twenty Five-130°F (5two-54°C) for three-four minutes per side.

• **Medium:** Grill at 13five-140°F (5seven-60°C) for four-five minutes per side.

2. **Shrimp:** Grill at 120-130°F (49-54°C) for two-three minutes per side until they turn pink.

3. **Tuna:** Grill at 1Twenty Five-130°F (5two-54°C) for two-three minutes per side for medium-rare.

4. **Scallops:** Grill at 120-130°F (49-54°C) for two-three minutes per side until they turn opaque.

5. **Whitefish:** Grill at 13five-140°F (5seven-60°C) for three-four minutes per side.

Keep in mind that these temperature guidelines are general recommendations. The actual grilling time may vary based on factors such as the thickness of the meat, the grill's heat, and your desired level of doneness. Always use a meat thermometer to ensure your meat reaches a safe internal temperature, especially for poultry.

• **Internal Temperatures for Meats**

Ensuring that your meat reaches the right internal temperature is essential for food safety and achieving the desired level of doneness. Here are the recommended internal temperatures for various types of meats:

Beef:

1. **Steak:**

• **Rare:** 125°F (52°C)

• **Medium-Rare:** 135°F (57°C)

• **Medium:** 145°F (63°C)

- **Medium-Well:** 155°F (68°C)

- **Well-Done:** 160°F (71°C)

2. **Ground Beef (Burgers):**

- **Medium-Rare:** 130°F (54°C)

- **Medium:** 140°F (60°C)

- **Medium-Well:** 150°F (66°C)

- **Well-Done:** 160°F (71°C)

3. **Roasts:**

- **Rare:** 120-130°F (49-54°C)

- **Medium-Rare:** 130-140°F (5four-60°C)

- **Medium:** 140-150°F (60-66°C)

- **Medium-Well:** 150-160°F (6six-71°C)

- **Well-Done:** 160°F (71°C) and above

Pork:

1. **Pork Chops:**

- **Medium-Rare:** 135°F (57°C)

- **Medium:** 145°F (63°C)

- **Medium-Well:** 150°F (66°C)

2. **Pork Tenderloin:**

- **Medium-Rare:** 140°F (60°C)

- **Medium:** 145°F (63°C)

- **Medium-Well:** 150°F (66°C)

3. **Pork Shoulder (Pulled Pork):**

- **Pulled Pork:** 19five-205°F (90-96°C)

Poultry:

1. **Chicken Breasts:**

- **Boneless, Skinless:** 165°F (74°C)

- **Bone-In, Skin-On:** 165°F (74°C)

2. **Chicken Thighs:**

- **Boneless, Skinless:** 165°F (74°C)

- **Bone-In, Skin-On:** 165°F (74°C)

3. **Whole Chicken (Spatchcocked):**

- **165°F (74°C)

Fish:

1. **Salmon:**

- **Medium-Rare:** 1Twenty Five-130°F (5two-54°C)

- **Medium:** 13five-140°F (5seven-60°C)

2. **Tuna:**

- **Medium-Rare:** 1Twenty Five-130°F (5two-54°C)

3. **Shrimp:**

- **Cook until they turn pink and opaque.**

4. **Scallops:**

- **Cook until they turn opaque.**

5. **Whitefish:**

- **Medium:** 13five-140°F (5seven-60°C)

Always use a reliable meat thermometer to check the internal temperature of your meat. Insert the thermometer into the thickest part of the meat, avoiding bones and fat, to get an accurate reading. By following these internal temperature guidelines, you'll ensure that your meats are not only safe to eat but also perfectly cooked to your desired level of doneness.

CHAPTER 7:
TIPS AND TRICKS

Enhancing the flavors of your griddled dishes often comes down to the sauces, spices, and seasonings you use. Here are some tips and recommendations to help you elevate your griddling game with the best flavor-enhancing **Ingredients:**

Sauces:

1.   **Barbecue Sauce:** Barbecue sauce is a griddling classic, and you can find various regional styles, from smoky to sweet and tangy. Brush it on ribs, chicken, or burgers during the final minutes of cooking for a flavorful glaze.

2.   **Teriyaki Sauce:** Teriyaki sauce adds a sweet and savory twist to griddled dishes. Use it to marinate chicken, beef, or salmon before grilling for a taste of the Pacific.

3.   **Hot Sauce:** Whether it's classic hot sauce or a unique hot pepper sauce, a dash can provide a spicy kick to your griddled foods. Add it to marinades, drizzle it on tacos, or use it as a condiment for a spicy finish.

4.   **Chimichurri:** Chimichurri is a vibrant herb sauce that pairs perfectly with grilled meats. Its bright, zesty flavors make it an excellent accompaniment for steaks, pork, and chicken.

5.   **Soy Sauce:** Soy sauce is a versatile and umami-rich option for marinating and seasoning your griddled dishes. Combine it with garlic, ginger, and sesame oil for a tasty Asian-inspired marinade.

Spices and Seasonings:

1.   **Garlic Powder:** Garlic powder is a pantry essential that adds a savory, aromatic flavor to meats, vegetables, and potatoes. Sprinkle it on your griddle creations before or after cooking.

2. **Smoked Paprika:** Smoked paprika imparts a smoky, earthy taste and a lovely red hue. It's ideal for seasoning burgers, roasted vegetables, and even popcorn for a unique twist.

3. **Cayenne Pepper:** A little cayenne pepper goes a long way in adding heat to your dishes. Use it sparingly to create a spicy kick in rubs or marinades.

4. **Cumin:** Cumin offers a warm, earthy flavor that's perfect for griddled Mexican and Tex-Mex dishes. Combine it with chili powder for a flavorful fajita or taco seasoning.

5. **Rosemary:** Fresh or dried rosemary is a fragrant herb that pairs well with grilled lamb, chicken, and potatoes. Brush meat with olive oil and sprinkle rosemary for a savory aroma.

6. **Cilantro:** Fresh cilantro leaves are a staple in many dishes, adding a bright, citrusy note. Use it as a garnish for tacos, grilled seafood, and salsas.

Seasoning Blends:

1. **Montreal Steak Seasoning:** This classic blend typically includes salt, black pepper, garlic, and paprika. It's an excellent choice for grilling steaks and other meats.

2. **Lemon Pepper Seasoning:** Lemon pepper seasoning combines zesty lemon with pungent black pepper. It's great for poultry, seafood, and vegetables.

3. **Cajun Seasoning:** Cajun seasoning brings a bold mix of spices, including cayenne, paprika, and garlic, for a lively kick. It's perfect for blackened dishes and seafood boils.

4. **Greek Seasoning:** Greek seasoning is a delightful blend of Mediterranean herbs and spices like oregano, thyme, and garlic. It pairs well with grilled lamb, chicken, and vegetables.

5. **Taco Seasoning:** Taco seasoning is a convenient blend of chili powder, cumin, and other spices. It's perfect for griddling ground beef or chicken for tacos and burritos.

Experiment with these sauces, spices, and seasonings to create a wide variety of flavors on your griddle. Combine them in unique ways and let your taste buds guide you to discover new and exciting flavor profiles for your griddled dishes.

- ## Using Sugar Sauces Effectively

Sugar-based sauces can add sweetness and caramelization to your griddled dishes, but using them effectively requires some know-how. Here are tips and tricks for using sugar sauces to enhance your griddling experience:

1. Selecting the Right Sugar Sauces:

- **Honey:** Honey is a versatile sweetener that can be used to glaze chicken, pork, or vegetables. Its natural sweetness and floral notes add depth to your dishes.

- **Maple Syrup:** Maple syrup provides a distinct, rich sweetness and is a classic choice for drizzling over pancakes and waffles on the griddle. It's also great for glazing bacon or ham.

- **Brown Sugar:** Brown sugar adds a molasses-like sweetness and can be used to create sweet rubs for meats or to caramelize fruits on the griddle.

- **Agave Nectar:** Agave nectar is a mild, low-glycemic sweetener that works well for marinating meats, sweetening dressings, or drizzling over grilled fruits.

2. Applying Sugar Sauces:

- **Glazing:** Use sugar sauces to create a shiny, caramelized glaze on your griddled dishes. Brush the sauce on meat, poultry, or vegetables during the last few minutes of cooking. The heat of the griddle will help the sauce caramelize.

- **Marinating:** Sugar sauces can also be used in marinades. Mix your chosen sauce with other flavorings like garlic, soy sauce, or herbs and marinate your meat for a few hours or overnight before grilling.

- **Drizzling:** Drizzle sugar sauces over grilled fruit, pancakes, or desserts. The heat from the griddle will enhance the sauce's flavors and create a luscious finish.

3. Avoiding Burning:

- Sugar sauces can easily burn on a hot griddle due to their high sugar content. To prevent burning, make sure your griddle is at a medium heat level, especially when glazing or drizzling.

- Pay close attention to the sauce as it cooks, and turn the food often to prevent excessive caramelization. If you notice the sauce darkening too quickly, move the food to a cooler area of the griddle.

4. Combining Sweet and Savory:

- Sugar sauces can create a delightful balance when combined with savory elements. For example, try mixing soy sauce, garlic, and brown sugar for a savory-sweet glaze.

- Incorporate sugar sauces into dishes like teriyaki chicken, honey-glazed ham, or maple bacon for a harmonious blend of sweet and savory flavors.

5. Cleaning Your Griddle:

- After using sugar sauces, it's essential to clean your griddle thoroughly to prevent the buildup of sticky residue. Use a grill brush or scraper to remove any caramelized sauce, and then wipe the surface with a damp cloth.

Using sugar sauces effectively on the griddle adds a delightful dimension to your dishes. By choosing the right sauces, applying them skillfully, and paying attention to heat levels, you can achieve a perfect balance of sweetness and savory flavors in your griddled creations.

- ### Eco-Friendly Griddling Tips

Griddling can be not only a delicious way to prepare meals but also an eco-friendly one. By following these tips, you can reduce your environmental impact and make your griddling experience more sustainable:

1. Choose Sustainable Ingredients:

- Opt for sustainably sourced meats, seafood, and vegetables. Look for eco-friendly certifications such as organic, grass-fed, or MSC-certified (for seafood) to support responsible farming and fishing practices.

2. Reduce Food Waste:

- Plan your meals and portion sizes to minimize food waste. If you have leftovers, repurpose them into new dishes or freeze them for later use.

3. Use Eco-Friendly Cooking Utensils:

• Invest in griddle utensils and accessories made from sustainable materials, such as bamboo or stainless steel, which are durable and have a lower environmental impact.

4. Energy-Efficient Griddling:

• Opt for energy-efficient griddle models that consume less power. Preheat your griddle only when you're ready to cook, and turn it off immediately after use.

5. Local and Seasonal Ingredients:

• Choose local and seasonal ingredients to reduce the environmental footprint associated with transportation and refrigeration. Farmer's markets and community-supported agriculture (CSA) programs are great sources for fresh, local produce.

6. Eco-Friendly Cleaners:

• Use environmentally friendly cleaning products to maintain your griddle. These cleaners are less harmful to the environment and your health.

7. Sustainable Fuels:

• If you're using a gas or propane griddle, consider switching to natural gas, which is a cleaner-burning fuel with fewer emissions.

8. Composting:

• Compost your food scraps, such as vegetable peels and trimmings. Compost can enrich your garden soil and reduce the amount of waste sent to landfills.

9. Reusable Cookware:

• Use reusable and eco-friendly cookware, such as cast iron or stainless steel griddles, which have long lifespans and reduce the need for disposable or non-stick cookware.

10. Water Conservation:

• Be mindful of water usage when cleaning your griddle. Use a spray bottle with water and a cloth to wipe down the surface, minimizing water waste.

11. Recycle and Dispose Properly:

• Recycle materials such as aluminum foil, griddle accessories, and packaging when possible. Dispose of used propane canisters and other grilling-related waste according to your local recycling guidelines.

12. Ditch Disposables:

• Avoid single-use plates, utensils, and napkins. Opt for reusable or biodegradable alternatives.

13. Responsible Charcoal Use:

• If you use a charcoal griddle, choose natural lump charcoal over briquettes, which often contain additives. Also, consider using a chimney starter for a more efficient and eco-friendly way to light charcoal.

By implementing these eco-friendly griddling practices, you can enjoy your outdoor cooking while minimizing your impact on the environment. These small changes can add up to make a positive difference in the long run.

CHAPTER 8:
BREAKFAST

1. Classic American Breakfast

Ingredients:

- four eggs

- four slices of bacon

- four breakfast sausages

- two cupful hash browns

- Salt and pepper to taste

Instructions:

1.   Preheat your Blackstone griddle to medium-high heat.

2.   Place the bacon and sausages on the griddle and cook until crispy and browned, turning occasionally. This takes about eight-ten minutes.

3.   Remove the bacon and sausages and keep them warm.

4.   Add the hash browns to the griddle and cook until they are golden brown and crispy, about eight-ten minutes. Season with salt and pepper.

5.   In the meantime, cook the eggs on the griddle to your desired level of doneness.

6.   Serve the eggs, bacon, sausages, and hash browns together for a classic American breakfast.

Duration: Approximately 20 minutes

Nutrients (per portion):

- Caloric content: 550

- Amino content: 25g

- Carb content: 25g

- Fatty acid: 40g

2. Blueberry Pancakes

Ingredients:

- one cupful all-purpose flour

- two tablespoonful sugar

- one teaspoonful baking powder

- half teaspoonful baking soda

- one-fourth teaspoonful salt

- one cupful buttermilk

- one egg

- two tablespoonful melted butter

- half cupful fresh blueberries

Instructions:

1. Preheat your griddle to medium-high heat.

2. In a mixing bowl, combine the flour, sugar, baking powder, baking soda, and salt.

3. In another bowl, whisk together the buttermilk, egg, and melted butter.

4. Pour the wet ingredients into the dry ingredients and stir until just combined.

5. Gently fold in the fresh blueberries.

6. Grease the griddle with a little butter or oil. Pour one-fourth cupful of pancake batter onto the griddle for each pancake.

7. Cook until bubbles form on the surface, then flip and cook until golden brown.

8. Serve with maple syrup and additional blueberries.

Duration: Approximately fifteen minutes

Nutrients (***per portion***, *two pancakes):*

- Caloric content: 220

- Amino content: 5g

- Carb content: 33g

- Fatty acid: 7g

3. Veggie Omelette

Ingredients:

- three eggs

- one-fourth cupful bell peppers, diced

- one-fourth cupful onion, diced

- one-fourth cupful tomatoes, diced

- one-fourth cupful mushrooms, sliced

- Salt and pepper to taste

- two tablespoonful grated cheddar cheese

Instructions:

1. Preheat the griddle to medium heat.

2. In a bowl, beat the eggs and season with salt and pepper.

3. Pour the eggs onto the griddle and quickly spread them into a large circle.

4. Sprinkle the bell peppers, onions, tomatoes, and mushrooms evenly over the eggs.

5. When the edges of the omelette start to set, carefully fold it in half.

6. Sprinkle the grated cheddar cheese on top.

7. Cook for an additional minute until the cheese is melted.

Duration: Approximately five minutes

Nutrients (per portion):

- Caloric content: 190

- Amino content: 15g

- Carb content: 7g

- Fatty acid: 11g

4. Breakfast Burritos

Ingredients:

- four large flour tortillas

- six eggs

- half cupful cooked breakfast sausage, crumbled

- one-fourth cupful diced bell peppers

- one-fourth cupful diced onions

- one-fourth cupful diced tomatoes

- one-fourth cupful shredded cheddar cheese

- Salt and pepper to taste

- Salsa and sour cream (optional, for serving)

Instructions:

1. Preheat your griddle to medium-high heat.

2. Scramble the eggs on the griddle, incorporating the cooked sausage, bell peppers, onions, and tomatoes. Season with salt and pepper.

3. Lay out the flour tortillas on a clean surface.

4. Spoon the egg mixture onto each tortilla and sprinkle with cheddar cheese.

5. Fold in the sides and roll up the tortillas to create burritos.

6. Place the burritos seam-side down on the griddle to crisp and warm them, turning occasionally. This takes about three-four minutes.

7. Serve with salsa and sour cream if desired.

Duration: Approximately fifteen minutes

Nutrients *(per burrito):*

- Caloric content: 450

- Amino content: 22g

- Carb content: 28g

- Fatty acid: 28g

5. Banana Pancakes

Ingredients:

- one cupful all-purpose flour

- two tablespoonful sugar

- one teaspoonful baking powder

- half teaspoonful baking soda

- one-fourth teaspoonful salt

- one cupful buttermilk

- one egg

- two tablespoonful melted butter

- one ripe banana, mashed

Instructions:

1. Preheat your griddle to medium-high heat.

2. In a mixing bowl, combine the flour, sugar, baking powder, baking soda, and salt.

3. In another bowl, whisk together the buttermilk, egg, melted butter, and mashed banana.

4. Pour the wet ingredients into the dry ingredients and stir until just combined.

5. Grease the griddle with a little butter or oil. Pour one-fourth cupful of pancake batter onto the griddle for each pancake.

6. Cook until bubbles form on the surface, then flip and cook until golden brown.

7. Serve with sliced bananas and a drizzle of honey.

Duration: Approximately fifteen minutes

Nutrients (per portion, two pancakes):

- Caloric content: 240

- Amino content: 5g

- Carb content: 38g

- Fatty acid: 7g

6. Breakfast Quesadillas

Ingredients:

- two large flour tortillas

- four eggs

- half cupful cooked bacon, crumbled

- one-fourth cupful diced bell peppers

- one-fourth cupful diced onions

- half cupful shredded cheddar cheese

- Salt and pepper to taste

- Salsa and sour cream (optional, for serving)

Instructions:

1. Preheat the griddle to medium-high heat.

2. Scramble the eggs on the griddle, incorporating the cooked bacon, bell peppers, and onions. Season with salt and pepper.

3. Lay out the flour tortillas on a clean surface.

4. Sprinkle half of the cheddar cheese evenly on one side of each tortilla.

5. Spoon the egg mixture onto the cheese side of one tortilla.

6. Place the other tortilla on top, cheese-side down, to create a quesadilla.

7. Cook on the griddle until the tortillas are crisp and the cheese is melted, about two-three minutes per side.

8. Cut the quesadilla into wedges and serve with salsa and sour cream.

Duration: Approximately ten minutes

Nutrients (per quesadilla):

- Caloric content: 550

- Amino content: 26g

- Carb content: 23g

- Fatty acid: 41g

7. Avocado Toast with Poached Eggs

Ingredients:

- two slices of whole-grain bread

- one ripe avocado

- two eggs

- Salt and pepper to taste

- Red pepper flakes (optional, for added spice)

- Chopped fresh cilantro or parsley for garnish

Instructions:

1. Preheat your griddle to medium-high heat.

2. Halve and pit the avocado. Scoop out the flesh into a bowl and mash it with a fork. Season with salt, pepper, and red pepper flakes if desired.

3. Toast the slices of whole-grain bread on the griddle until they are lightly browned.

4. Poach the eggs on the griddle: Fill a pan with about an inch of water and bring it to a gentle simmer. Crack each egg into a small bowl and then gently slide it into the simmering water. Poach for about three-four minutes until the whites are set, but the yolks are still runny.

5. Spread the mashed avocado on the toasted bread slices and top each with a poached egg.

6. Garnish with chopped cilantro or parsley and season with additional salt and pepper.

Duration: Approximately ten minutes

Nutrients (per portion):

- Caloric content: 350

- Amino content: 12g

- Carb content: 28g

- Fatty acid: 22g

8. Greek Yogurt Parfait

Ingredients:

- one cupful Greek yogurt

- half cupful granola

- half cupful mixed berries (strawberries, blueberries, raspberries)

- Honey for drizzling

Instructions:

1. Preheat your griddle to medium heat.

2. In a bowl or glass, layer Greek yogurt, granola, and mixed berries.

3. Drizzle honey over the top for added sweetness.

4. Serve the parfait for a healthy and quick breakfast.

Duration: No cooking required

Nutrients (per portion):

- Caloric content: 350

- Amino content: 17g

- Carb content: 45g

- Fatty acid: 12g

9. Huevos Rancheros

Ingredients:

- two corn tortillas

- two eggs

- half cupful black beans, cooked and mashed

- one-fourth cupful salsa

- one-fourth cupful diced onions

- one-fourth cupful shredded cheddar cheese

- Salt and pepper to taste

- Fresh cilantro for garnish

Instructions:

1. Preheat the griddle to medium-high heat.

2. Warm the corn tortillas on the griddle until they are pliable and slightly toasted.

3. Cook the eggs on the griddle to your desired level of doneness.

4. Spread the mashed black beans on each tortilla.

5. Place a cooked egg on top of the beans on each tortilla.

6. Spoon salsa over the eggs and sprinkle with diced onions, cheddar cheese, salt, and pepper.

7. Garnish with fresh cilantro.

Duration: Approximately ten minutes

Nutrients (per portion):

- Caloric content: 350

- Amino content: 16g

- Carb content: 30g

- Fatty acid: 19g

10. Smoked Salmon and Cream Cheese Bagel

Ingredients:

- two bagels

- four oz smoked salmon

- four oz cream cheese

- one-fourth cupful red onion, thinly sliced

- two tablespoonful capers

- Fresh dill for garnish

Instructions:

1. Preheat the griddle to medium heat.

2. Cut the bagels in half and toast them on the griddle until they are lightly browned.

3. Spread cream cheese on each bagel half.

4. Arrange smoked salmon on top of the cream cheese.

5. Sprinkle red onion slices and capers over the salmon.

6. Garnish with fresh dill.

Duration: Approximately five minutes

Nutrients (per portion):

- Caloric content: 380

- Amino content: 18g

- Carb content: 39g

- Fatty acid: 17g

CHAPTER 9:
TEX-MEX TACOS AND MORE

1. Steak Fajitas

Ingredients:

- one lb flank steak

- one red bell pepper, sliced

- one green bell pepper, sliced

- one red onion, sliced

- two tablespoonful fajita seasoning

- Flour tortillas

- Sour cream, guacamole, and salsa for serving

Instructions:

1. Preheat your griddle to medium-high heat.

2. Season the flank steak with fajita seasoning and grill for four-five minutes per side, or to your desired level of doneness.

3. In a separate area of the griddle, sauté the sliced bell peppers and red onion until they are tender and slightly caramelized.

4. Slice the steak into thin strips.

5. Serve the steak and sautéed vegetables in flour tortillas with sour cream, guacamole, and salsa.

Duration: Approximately fifteen minutes

Nutrients (per portion):

- Caloric content: 350

- Amino content: 30g

- Carb content: 25g

- Fatty acid: 15g

2. Chicken Tacos

Ingredients:

- one lb boneless, skinless chicken thighs

- two tablespoonful taco seasoning

- eight small corn tortillas

- one cupful shredded lettuce

- one cupful diced tomatoes

- half cupful shredded cheddar cheese

- one-fourth cupful diced red onions

- Salsa and sour cream for serving

Instructions:

1. Preheat your griddle to medium-high heat.

2. Season the chicken thighs with taco seasoning and grill for five-six minutes per side, or until fully cooked.

3. Slice the grilled chicken into thin strips.

4. Warm the corn tortillas on the griddle until they are pliable.

5. Assemble the tacos by filling each tortilla with shredded lettuce, diced tomatoes, grilled chicken, shredded cheddar cheese, and diced red onions.

6. Serve with salsa and sour cream.

Duration: Approximately fifteen minutes

Nutrients (*per portion*, *two tacos):*

- Caloric content: 350

- Amino content: 28g

- Carb content: 28g

- Fatty acid: 15g

3. Shrimp Tacos

Ingredients:

- one lb large shrimp, peeled and deveined

- two tablespoonful taco seasoning

- eight small flour tortillas

- one cupful shredded cabbage

- half cupful diced tomatoes

- one-fourth cupful chopped cilantro

- Lime wedges and hot sauce for serving

Instructions:

1. Preheat your griddle to medium-high heat.

2. Season the shrimp with taco seasoning and grill for two-three minutes per side, or until they turn pink and opaque.

3. Warm the flour tortillas on the griddle until they are pliable.

4. Assemble the tacos by filling each tortilla with shredded cabbage, diced tomatoes, grilled shrimp, and chopped cilantro.

5. Serve with lime wedges and hot sauce.

Duration: Approximately ten minutes

Nutrients (per portion, *two tacos):*

- Caloric content: 280

- Amino content: 25g

- Carb content: 30g

- Fatty acid: 6g

4. Veggie Quesadillas

Ingredients:

- four large flour tortillas

- two cupful shredded Monterey Jack cheese

- one cupful sliced bell peppers

- one cupful sliced onions

- one cupful sliced mushrooms

- one cupful baby spinach leaves

- Salsa and sour cream for serving

Instructions:

1. Preheat your griddle to medium heat.

2. Lay out two tortillas and sprinkle half of the shredded cheese on each.

3. Distribute the sliced bell peppers, onions, mushrooms, and baby spinach over the cheese.

4. Place the remaining tortillas on top to create quesadillas.

5. Cook on the griddle until the tortillas are crispy and the cheese is melted, about three-four minutes per side.

6. Slice into wedges and serve with salsa and sour cream.

Duration: Approximately ten minutes

Nutrients (*per portion*, *one quesadilla):*

- Caloric content: 400

- Amino content: 15g

- Carb content: 25g

- Fatty acid: 25g

5. Black Bean and Corn Tacos

Ingredients:

- one can (fifteen oz) black beans, drained and rinsed

- one cupful corn kernels (fresh or frozen)

- half cupful diced red bell pepper

- one-fourth cupful chopped cilantro

- one teaspoonful cumin

- half teaspoonful chili powder

- eight small corn tortillas

- Salsa and sliced avocado for serving

Instructions:

1. Preheat your griddle to medium-high heat.

2. In a large bowl, mix the black beans, corn, diced red bell pepper, cilantro, cumin, and chili powder.

3. Warm the corn tortillas on the griddle until they are pliable.

4. Assemble the tacos by filling each tortilla with the black bean and corn mixture.

5. Serve with salsa and sliced avocado.

Duration: Approximately ten minutes

Nutrients (*per portion*, *two tacos):*

- Caloric content: 350

- Amino content: 10g

- Carb content: 65g

- Fatty acid: 5g

6. Beef and Bean Burritos

Ingredients:

- one lb ground beef

- one can (fifteen oz) refried beans

- half cupful diced onions

- two tablespoonful taco seasoning

- eight large flour tortillas

- one cupful shredded cheddar cheese

- Sour cream and guacamole for serving

Instructions:

1. Preheat your griddle to medium-high heat.

2. In a skillet on the griddle, cook the ground beef and onions until the beef is browned. Drain any excess fat.

3. Stir in the refried beans and taco seasoning, and cook for an additional two-three minutes.

4. Warm the flour tortillas on the griddle until they are pliable.

5. Assemble the burritos by filling each tortilla with the beef and bean mixture, shredded cheddar cheese, and a dollop of sour cream and guacamole.

6. Roll up the burritos, tucking in the sides.

Duration: Approximately fifteen minutes

Nutrients (*per burrito*):

*   Caloric content: 550

*   Amino content: 25g

*   Carb content: 45g

*   Fatty acid: 30g

7. Baja Fish Tacos

Ingredients:

*   one lb white fish fillets (such as cod or tilapia)

*   one cupful all-purpose flour

*   half cupful cold water

*   half cupful beer

*   one teaspoonful baking powder

*   half teaspoonful salt

*   eight small flour tortillas

*   Shredded cabbage

*   Sliced jalapeños

- Lime wedges and tartar sauce for serving

Instructions:

1. Preheat your griddle to medium-high heat.

2. In a mixing bowl, whisk together the flour, cold water, beer, baking powder, and salt to create the beer batter.

3. Dip the fish fillets in the beer batter and place them on the griddle. Cook for three-four minutes per side, or until the fish is crispy and cooked through.

4. Warm the flour tortillas on the griddle until they are pliable.

5. Assemble the tacos by filling each tortilla with shredded cabbage, sliced jalapeños, and a beer-battered fish fillet.

6. Serve with lime wedges and tartar sauce.

Duration: Approximately fifteen minutes

Nutrients (per portion, two tacos):

- Caloric content: 450

- Amino content: 20g

- Carb content: 60g

- Fatty acid: 12g

8. Griddled Queso Fundido

Ingredients:

- one cupful shredded Oaxaca or Monterey Jack cheese

- half cupful crumbled Mexican chorizo

- one-fourth cupful diced tomatoes

- two tablespoonful chopped cilantro

- four small corn tortillas

Instructions:

1. Preheat your griddle to medium heat.

2. In a cast iron skillet on the griddle, heat the chorizo until it's fully cooked and slightly crispy.

3. Sprinkle the shredded cheese evenly over the chorizo.

4. Once the cheese starts to melt, sprinkle diced tomatoes and chopped cilantro on top.

5. Warm the corn tortillas on the griddle until they are pliable.

6. Scoop the melted cheese mixture onto each tortilla.

7. Fold the tortillas in half to create quesadillas.

Duration: Approximately ten minutes

Nutrients (*per portion*, *two quesadillas*):

- Caloric content: 380

- Amino content: 16g

- Carb content: 20g

- Fatty acid: 25g

9. Breakfast Tacos

Ingredients:

- half lb breakfast sausage

- four large eggs

- half cupful diced bell peppers

- half cupful diced onions

- eight small flour tortillas

- Salsa and shredded cheddar cheese for serving

Instructions:

1. Preheat your griddle to medium-high heat.

2. Cook the breakfast sausage on the griddle until browned and crumbled.

3. In a separate area of the griddle, scramble the eggs with diced bell peppers and onions until fully cooked.

4. Warm the flour tortillas on the griddle until they are pliable.

5. Assemble the tacos by filling each tortilla with a portion of scrambled eggs and breakfast sausage.

6. Serve with salsa and shredded cheddar cheese.

Duration: Approximately fifteen minutes

Nutrients (per portion, *two tacos):*

- Caloric content: 450

- Amino content: 18g

- Carb content: 35g

- Fatty acid: 26g

10. Griddled Quesadilla Burger

Ingredients:

- one lb ground beef

- one tablespoonful taco seasoning

- four small flour tortillas

- one cupful shredded cheddar cheese

- half cupful diced tomatoes

- one-fourth cupful diced onions

- Salsa and sour cream for serving

Instructions:

1. Preheat your griddle to medium-high heat.

2. Season the ground beef with taco seasoning and form it into burger patties.

3. Grill the burger patties for three-four minutes per side, or until they are cooked to your desired level.

4. Warm the flour tortillas on the griddle until they are pliable.

5. Assemble the quesadilla burger by placing a tortilla on the griddle, sprinkling shredded cheddar cheese, and then topping with a burger patty, diced tomatoes, and diced onions.

6. Place another tortilla on top, press gently, and grill for an additional two minutes per side to melt the cheese.

7. Serve with salsa and sour cream.

Duration: Approximately ten minutes

Nutrients (per portion):

- Caloric content: 550

- Amino content: 28g

- Carb content: 25g

- Fatty acid: 35g

CHAPTER 10:
BURGERS

1. Classic Cheeseburger

Ingredients:

- one lb ground beef (80% lean)

- four burger buns

- four slices of American cheese

- Lettuce, tomato, onion, and pickles for garnish

- Ketchup and mustard for condiments

Instructions:

1. Preheat your griddle to medium-high heat.

2. Divide the ground beef into four equal portions and shape them into burger patties.

3. Place the burger patties on the griddle and cook for three-four minutes per side, or until they reach your desired level of doneness.

4. During the last minute of cooking, add a slice of American cheese to each patty and let it melt.

5. Toast the burger buns on the griddle.

6. Assemble the burgers with lettuce, tomato, onion, pickles, ketchup, and mustard.

Duration: Approximately ten minutes

Nutrients (per portion):

- Caloric content: 450

- Amino content: 25g

- Carb content: 25g

- Fatty acid: 28g

2. Bacon BBQ Burger

Ingredients:

- one lb ground beef (80% lean)

- four burger buns

- four slices of cheddar cheese

- eight slices of bacon, cooked

- BBQ sauce

- Lettuce, tomato, and onion for garnish

Instructions:

1. Preheat your griddle to medium-high heat.

2. Divide the ground beef into four equal portions and shape them into burger patties.

3. Place the burger patties on the griddle and cook for three-four minutes per side, or until they reach your desired level of doneness.

4. During the last minute of cooking, add a slice of cheddar cheese to each patty and let it melt.

5. Toast the burger buns on the griddle.

6. Assemble the burgers with bacon, lettuce, tomato, onion, and a drizzle of BBQ sauce.

Duration: Approximately ten minutes

Nutrients (per portion):

- Caloric content: 520

- Amino content: 27g

- Carb content: 26g

- Fatty acid: 34g

3. Mushroom Swiss Burger

Ingredients:

- one lb ground beef (80% lean)

- four burger buns

- four slices of Swiss cheese

- two cupful sliced mushrooms

- two cloves garlic, minced

- Butter

- Lettuce and mayonnaise for garnish

Instructions:

1. Preheat your griddle to medium-high heat.

2. Divide the ground beef into four equal portions and shape them into burger patties.

3. Place the burger patties on the griddle and cook for three-four minutes per side, or until they reach your desired level of doneness.

4. During the last minute of cooking, add a slice of Swiss cheese to each patty and let it melt.

5. In a separate area of the griddle, melt butter and sauté the sliced mushrooms and minced garlic until they are tender.

6. Toast the burger buns on the griddle.

7. Assemble the burgers with sautéed mushrooms, lettuce, and a dollop of mayonnaise.

Duration: Approximately fifteen minutes

Nutrients (per portion):

- Caloric content: 480

- Amino content: 26g

- Carb content: 25g

- Fatty acid: 31g

4. Veggie Burger

Ingredients:

- four veggie burger patties (store-bought or homemade)

- four whole-grain burger buns

- Lettuce, tomato, onion, and avocado for garnish

- Mustard and ketchup for condiments

Instructions:

1. Preheat your griddle to medium-high heat.

2. Grill the veggie burger patties on the griddle for four-five minutes per side, or until they are heated through and have grill marks.

3. Toast the whole-grain burger buns on the griddle.

4. Assemble the veggie burgers with lettuce, tomato, onion, avocado, and condiments of your choice.

Duration: Approximately ten minutes

Nutrients (per portion):

- Caloric content: 320

- Amino content: 10g

- Carb content: 40g

- Fatty acid: 14g

5. Jalapeño Popper Burger

Ingredients:

- one lb ground beef (80% lean)

- four burger buns

- four slices of cream cheese

- four slices of pickled jalapeños

- eight slices of bacon, cooked

- Lettuce and mayonnaise for garnish

Instructions:

1. Preheat your griddle to medium-high heat.

2. Divide the ground beef into four equal portions and shape them into burger patties.

3. Place the burger patties on the griddle and cook for three-four minutes per side, or until they reach your desired level of doneness.

4. During the last minute of cooking, add a slice of cream cheese and a pickled jalapeño to each patty.

5. Toast the burger buns on the griddle.

6. Assemble the burgers with bacon, lettuce, and a dollop of mayonnaise.

Duration: Approximately ten minutes

Nutrients (per portion):

- Caloric content: 480

- Amino content: 25g

- Carb content: 25g

- Fatty acid: 30g

6. Teriyaki Pineapple Burger

Ingredients:

- one lb ground beef (80% lean)

- four burger buns

- four pineapple rings

- Teriyaki sauce

- Lettuce and red onion for garnish

Instructions:

1. Preheat your griddle to medium-high heat.

2. Divide the ground beef into four equal portions and shape them into burger patties.

3. Place the burger patties on the griddle and cook for three-four minutes per side, or until they reach your desired level of doneness.

4. During the last minute of cooking, brush each patty with teriyaki sauce.

5. Grill the pineapple rings on the griddle for about two minutes per side, until they have grill marks.

6. Toast the burger buns on the griddle.

7. Assemble the burgers with teriyaki-glazed patties, grilled pineapple rings, lettuce, and red onion.

Duration: Approximately fifteen minutes

Nutrients (per portion):

- Caloric content: 440

- Amino content: 26g

- Carb content: 30g

- Fatty acid: 25g

7. BBQ Bacon Ranch Burger

Ingredients:

- one lb ground beef (80% lean)
- four burger buns
- four slices of bacon, cooked
- BBQ sauce
- Ranch dressing
- Lettuce and tomato for garnish

Instructions:

1. Preheat your griddle to medium-high heat.

2. Divide the ground beef into four equal portions and shape them into burger patties.

3. Place the burger patties on the griddle and cook for three-four minutes per side, or until they reach your desired level of doneness.

4. During the last minute of cooking, brush each patty with BBQ sauce.

5. Toast the burger buns on the griddle.

6. Assemble the burgers with bacon, lettuce, tomato, a drizzle of ranch dressing, and additional BBQ sauce if desired.

Duration: Approximately ten minutes

Nutrients (per portion):

- Caloric content: 490
- Amino content: 27g
- Carb content: 25g

- Fatty acid: 31g

8. Guacamole Turkey Burger

Ingredients:

- one lb ground turkey

- four burger buns

- one cupful guacamole

- Lettuce and red onion for garnish

- Salsa for condiments

Instructions:

1. Preheat your griddle to medium-high heat.

2. Divide the ground turkey into four equal portions and shape them into burger patties.

3. Place the turkey burger patties on the griddle and cook for four-five minutes per side, or until they are fully cooked.

4. Toast the burger buns on the griddle.

5. Assemble the burgers with a generous scoop of guacamole, lettuce, red onion, and a dollop of salsa.

Duration: Approximately ten minutes

Nutrients (per portion):

- Caloric content: 350

- Amino content: 20g

- Carb content: 30g

- Fatty acid: 16g

9. Blue Cheese Buffalo Burger

Ingredients:

- one lb ground beef (80% lean)

- four burger buns

- four tablespoonful buffalo sauce

- half cupful crumbled blue cheese

- Lettuce and tomato for garnish

Instructions:

1.   Preheat your griddle to medium-high heat.

2.   Divide the ground beef into four equal portions and shape them into burger patties.

3.   Place the burger patties on the griddle and cook for three-four minutes per side, or until they reach your desired level of doneness.

4.   During the last minute of cooking, drizzle one tablespoon of buffalo sauce on each patty and top with crumbled blue cheese.

5.   Toast the burger buns on the griddle.

6.   Assemble the burgers with lettuce, tomato, and additional buffalo sauce if desired.

Duration: Approximately ten minutes

Nutrients (per portion):

- Caloric content: 480

- Amino content: 26g

- Carb content: 25g

- Fatty acid: 30g

10. Hawaiian Teriyaki Burger

Ingredients:

- one lb ground beef (80% lean)

- four burger buns

- four pineapple rings

- Teriyaki sauce

- Lettuce and red onion for garnish

Instructions:

1. Preheat your griddle to medium-high heat.

2. Divide the ground beef into four equal portions and shape them into burger patties.

3. Place the burger patties on the griddle and cook for three-four minutes per side, or until they reach your desired level of doneness.

4. During the last minute of cooking, brush each patty with teriyaki sauce.

5. Grill the pineapple rings on the griddle for about two minutes per side, until they have grill marks.

6. Toast the burger buns on the griddle.

7. Assemble the burgers with teriyaki-glazed patties, grilled pineapple rings, lettuce, and red onion.

Duration: Approximately fifteen minutes

Nutrients (per portion):

- Caloric content: 450

- Amino content: 26g

- Carb content: 30g

- Fatty acid: 25g

CHAPTER 11:
FISH

1. Lemon Herb Grilled Salmon

Ingredients:

- four salmon fillets (six-eight oz each)

- two lemons, zested and juiced

- two cloves garlic, minced

- two tablespoonful fresh dill, chopped

- two tablespoonful olive oil

- Salt and pepper to taste

Instructions:

1. Preheat your griddle to medium-high heat.

2. In a bowl, mix together the lemon zest, lemon juice, minced garlic, chopped dill, and olive oil.

3. Season the salmon fillets with salt and pepper.

4. Brush the lemon herb mixture over the salmon fillets.

5. Grill the salmon on the griddle for about four-five minutes per side, or until the fish flakes easily with a fork.

Duration: Approximately ten minutes

Nutrients (per portion):

- Caloric content: 350

- Amino content: 35g

- Carb content: 4g

- Fatty acid: 21g

2. Teriyaki Glazed Mahi-Mahi

Ingredients:

- four mahi-mahi fillets (six-eight oz each)

- half cupful teriyaki sauce

- two tablespoonful brown sugar

- one teaspoonful ginger, minced

- one teaspoonful garlic, minced

- Sesame seeds for garnish

Instructions:

1. Preheat your griddle to medium-high heat.

2. In a bowl, mix together the teriyaki sauce, brown sugar, minced ginger, and minced garlic to create the glaze.

3. Season the mahi-mahi fillets with a bit of salt and pepper.

4. Grill the mahi-mahi on the griddle for about four-five minutes per side, brushing with the teriyaki glaze.

5. Sprinkle sesame seeds over the fish before serving.

Duration: Approximately ten minutes

Nutrients (per portion):

- Caloric content: 300

- Amino content: 30g

- Carb content: 18g

- Fatty acid: 10g

3. Lemon Butter Grilled Trout

Ingredients:

- four trout fillets (six-eight oz each)

- two lemons, sliced

- four tablespoonful butter

- two cloves garlic, minced

- two tablespoonful fresh parsley, chopped

- Salt and pepper to taste

Instructions:

1. Preheat your griddle to medium-high heat.

2. Season the trout fillets with salt and pepper.

3. Place a slice of lemon on each trout fillet.

4. In a small pan on the griddle, melt the butter and add minced garlic and chopped parsley.

5. Drizzle the lemon butter mixture over the trout fillets.

6. Grill the trout on the griddle for about four-five minutes per side, or until the fish is cooked through.

Duration: Approximately ten minutes

Nutrients (per portion):

- Caloric content: 320

- Amino content: 30g

- Carb content: 6g

- Fatty acid: 19g

4. Cajun Blackened Red Snapper

Ingredients:

- four red snapper fillets (six-eight oz each)

- two tablespoonful Cajun seasoning

- two tablespoonful olive oil

- Lemon wedges for serving

Instructions:

1. Preheat your griddle to high heat.

2. Brush the red snapper fillets with olive oil.

3. Coat both sides of the fillets with Cajun seasoning.

4. Grill the red snapper on the griddle for about three-four minutes per side, or until the fish is blackened and cooked through.

5. Serve with lemon wedges for a fresh squeeze of citrus.

Duration: Approximately eight minutes

Nutrients (per portion):

- Caloric content: 320

- Amino content: 35g

- Carb content: 5g

- Fatty acid: 18g

5. Garlic Parmesan Grilled Tilapia

Ingredients:

- four tilapia fillets (six-eight oz each)

- half cupful grated Parmesan cheese

- two cloves garlic, minced

- two tablespoonful fresh parsley, chopped

- two tablespoonful olive oil

- Salt and pepper to taste

Instructions:

1. Preheat your griddle to medium-high heat.

2. In a bowl, mix together the grated Parmesan cheese, minced garlic, chopped parsley, and olive oil.

3. Season the tilapia fillets with salt and pepper.

4. Brush the garlic Parmesan mixture over the tilapia fillets.

5. Grill the tilapia on the griddle for about three-four minutes per side, or until the fish flakes easily with a fork.

Duration: Approximately eight minutes

Nutrients (per portion):

- Caloric content: 280

- Amino content: 30g

- Carb content: 2g

- Fatty acid: 16g

6. Grilled Swordfish Steaks

Ingredients:

- four swordfish steaks (six-eight oz each)

- one-fourth cupful olive oil

- two tablespoonful lemon juice

- two teaspoonful dried oregano

- two cloves garlic, minced

- Salt and pepper to taste

Instructions:

1. Preheat your griddle to medium-high heat.

2. In a bowl, mix together the olive oil, lemon juice, dried oregano, minced garlic, salt, and pepper.

3. Brush the olive oil mixture over the swordfish steaks.

4. Grill the swordfish on the griddle for about four-five minutes per side, or until the fish is cooked through.

Duration: Approximately ten minutes

Nutrients (per portion):

- Caloric content: 350

- Amino content: 30g

- Carb content: 2g

- Fatty acid: 25g

7. Griddled Tuna Steaks

Ingredients:

- four tuna steaks (six-eight oz each)

- two tablespoonful sesame oil

- two tablespoonful soy sauce

- two teaspoonful ginger, minced

- two cloves garlic, minced

- Sesame seeds for garnish

Instructions:

1. Preheat your griddle to high heat.

2. In a bowl, mix together the sesame oil, soy sauce, minced ginger, and minced garlic.

3. Brush the sesame oil mixture over the tuna steaks.

4. Grill the tuna on the griddle for about two-three minutes per side, or until the fish is seared on the outside and still pink in the center.

5. Sprinkle sesame seeds over the fish before serving.

Duration: Approximately six minutes

Nutrients (per portion):

- Caloric content: 300

- Amino content: 40g

- Carb content: 3g

- Fatty acid: 13g

8. Coconut Shrimp Skewers

Ingredients:

- one lb large shrimp, peeled and deveined

- one cupful shredded coconut

- half cupful panko breadcrumbs

- one-fourth cupful all-purpose flour

- two eggs, beaten

- Salt and pepper to taste

- Sweet chili sauce for dipping

Instructions:

1. Preheat your griddle to medium-high heat.

2. In separate bowls, place the flour, beaten eggs, and a mixture of shredded coconut and panko breadcrumbs.

3. Season the shrimp with salt and pepper.

4. Thread the shrimp onto skewers.

5. Dip each shrimp skewer into the flour, then the beaten eggs, and finally into the coconut-panko mixture.

6. Grill the shrimp skewers on the griddle for about two-three minutes per side, or until they are golden brown and the shrimp is cooked through.

7. Serve with sweet chili sauce for dipping.

Duration: Approximately eight minutes

Nutrients (*per portion*, *four shrimp skewers):*

*   Caloric content: 320

*   Amino content: 20g

*   Carb content: 20g

*   Fatty acid: 18g

9. Griddled Scallops with Lemon Butter

Ingredients:

*   one lb sea scallops

*   two lemons, zested and juiced

*   four tablespoonful butter

*   two cloves garlic, minced

*   Salt and pepper to taste

- Fresh parsley for garnish

Instructions:

1. Preheat your griddle to medium-high heat.

2. Season the sea scallops with salt and pepper.

3. In a small pan on the griddle, melt the butter and add minced garlic, lemon zest, and lemon juice.

4. Grill the sea scallops on the griddle for about two-three minutes per side, or until they are opaque and slightly browned.

5. Drizzle the lemon butter sauce over the scallops and garnish with fresh parsley.

Duration: Approximately six minutes

Nutrients (per portion):

- Caloric content: 280

- Amino content: 20g

- Carb content: 7g

- Fatty acid: 18g

10. Griddled Catfish Po' Boys

Ingredients:

- four catfish fillets

- four French bread rolls

- one cupful shredded lettuce

- half cupful sliced pickles

- Remoulade sauce (mayo, mustard, hot sauce, and spices)

- two cupful cornmeal

- half cupful buttermilk

- one teaspoonful Cajun seasoning

- Vegetable oil for frying

Instructions:

1. Preheat your griddle to medium-high heat.

2. In a bowl, mix the cornmeal and Cajun seasoning.

3. Dip the catfish fillets in buttermilk and coat them with the cornmeal mixture.

4. Heat vegetable oil in a deep skillet or on the griddle.

5. Fry the catfish fillets for about three-four minutes per side, or until they are golden brown and cooked through.

6. Slice the French bread rolls and toast them on the griddle.

7. Assemble the po' boys with lettuce, fried catfish fillets, pickles, and remoulade sauce.

Duration: Approximately 1two minutes

Nutrients (per portion):

- Caloric content: 420

- Amino content: 25g

- Carb content: 35g

- Fatty acid: 18g

CHAPTER 12:
SANDWICHES

1. Classic Grilled Cheese Sandwich

Ingredients:

- eight slices of bread

- eight slices of American cheese

- Butter

Instructions:

1. Preheat your griddle to medium-high heat.

2. Butter one side of each slice of bread.

3. Place a slice of American cheese between two slices of bread, with the buttered side facing out.

4. Grill the sandwiches on the griddle for about two-three minutes per side, or until the bread is golden brown and the cheese is melted.

Duration: Approximately six minutes

Nutrients (per sandwich):

- Caloric content: 380

- Amino content: 14g

- Carb content: 30g

- Fatty acid: 23g

2. Philly Cheesesteak Sandwich

Ingredients:

- one lb thinly sliced ribeye steak
- two bell peppers, thinly sliced
- one onion, thinly sliced
- four slices of provolone cheese
- four sub rolls
- Salt and pepper to taste
- Olive oil

Instructions:

1. Preheat your griddle to medium-high heat.

2. Heat some olive oil on the griddle and sauté the sliced bell peppers and onions until they are tender. Remove from the griddle and set aside.

3. Season the ribeye steak with salt and pepper.

4. Grill the steak on the griddle for about two-three minutes per side, or until it's cooked to your desired level.

5. Place a slice of provolone cheese on each steak slice and let it melt.

6. Toast the sub rolls on the griddle.

7. Assemble the sandwiches with the steak, sautéed peppers and onions.

Duration: Approximately fifteen minutes

Nutrients (per sandwich):

- Caloric content: 480
- Amino content: 30g
- Carb content: 30g

- Fatty acid: 26g

3. Chicken Caprese Panini

Ingredients:

- two boneless, skinless chicken breasts

- four ciabatta rolls

- four slices of mozzarella cheese

- four slices of tomato

- Fresh basil leaves

- Balsamic glaze

- Olive oil

- Salt and pepper to taste

Instructions:

1. Preheat your griddle to medium-high heat.

2. Season the chicken breasts with salt, pepper, and a drizzle of olive oil.

3. Grill the chicken on the griddle for about six-seven minutes per side, or until they are cooked through.

4. Slice the ciabatta rolls in half and toast them on the griddle.

5. Assemble the paninis with grilled chicken, mozzarella cheese, tomato slices, fresh basil leaves, and a drizzle of balsamic glaze.

Duration: Approximately fifteen minutes

Nutrients (per panini):

- Caloric content: 380

- Amino content: 35g

- Carb content: 35g

- Fatty acid: 15g

4. Cubano Sandwich

Ingredients:

- one lb pork shoulder, slow-cooked and shredded

- four Cuban bread rolls or baguettes

- eight slices of ham

- eight slices of Swiss cheese

- Dill pickles

- Mustard

- Butter

Instructions:

1. Preheat your griddle to medium-high heat.

2. Slice the Cuban bread rolls or baguettes in half.

3. Spread mustard on one side of each roll.

4. Layer the shredded pork, ham, Swiss cheese, and dill pickles on the rolls.

5. Butter the outside of the rolls.

6. Grill the Cubano sandwiches on the griddle for about two-three minutes per side, or until the bread is crispy and the cheese is melted.

Duration: Approximately six minutes

Nutrients (per sandwich):

- Caloric content: 450

- Amino content: 28g

- Carb content: 30g

- Fatty acid: 24g

5. BBQ Pulled Pork Sandwich

Ingredients:

- one lb pulled pork

- four hamburger buns

- Coleslaw

- BBQ sauce

Instructions:

1. Preheat your griddle to medium-high heat.

2. Heat the pulled pork on the griddle, stirring with BBQ sauce until heated through.

3. Slice the hamburger buns and toast them on the griddle.

4. Assemble the sandwiches with pulled pork and coleslaw.

Duration: Approximately ten minutes

Nutrients (per sandwich):

- Caloric content: 400

- Amino content: 24g

- Carb content: 30g

- Fatty acid: 18g

6. Turkey and Avocado Wrap

Ingredients:

- four large tortillas

- one lb sliced turkey

- one avocado, sliced

- one cupful baby spinach leaves

- half cupful mayonnaise

- one tablespoonful Dijon mustard

Instructions:

1. Preheat your griddle to medium heat.

2. In a bowl, mix mayonnaise and Dijon mustard.

3. Spread the mayo-mustard mixture on each tortilla.

4. Layer sliced turkey, avocado, and baby spinach on each tortilla.

5. Wrap the tortillas tightly and grill on the griddle for about two minutes per side, or until they are warm and slightly crispy.

Duration: Approximately four minutes

Nutrients *(per wrap):*

- Caloric content: 380

- Amino content: 28g

- Carb content: 20g

- Fatty acid: 22g

7. Reuben Sandwich

Ingredients:

- eight slices of rye bread

- eight slices of corned beef

- eight slices of Swiss cheese

- one cupful sauerkraut, drained

- Thousand Island dressing

- Butter

Instructions:

1.   Preheat your griddle to medium-high heat.

2.   Butter one side of each slice of rye bread.

3.   Layer a slice of Swiss cheese, corned beef, sauerkraut, and another slice of Swiss cheese on each sandwich.

4.   Grill the sandwiches on the griddle for about three-four minutes per side, or until the bread is golden brown and the cheese is melted.

Duration: Approximately eight minutes

Nutrients *(per sandwich):*

- Caloric content: 450

- Amino content: 30g

- Carb content: 30g

- Fatty acid: 24g

8. BLT Wrap

Ingredients:

- four large tortillas

- one lb bacon, cooked

- two cupful shredded lettuce

- two tomatoes, sliced

- Mayonnaise

Instructions:

1. Preheat your griddle to medium heat.

2. Cook the bacon on the griddle until crispy, then drain on paper towels.

3. In each tortilla, spread a layer of mayonnaise.

4. Layer bacon, lettuce, and tomato slices on each tortilla.

5. Wrap the tortillas and grill on the griddle for about two minutes per side, or until they are warm and slightly crispy.

Duration: Approximately four minutes

Nutrients *(per wrap):*

- Caloric content: 380

- Amino content: 16g

- Carb content: 25g

- Fatty acid: 26g

9. Chicken Fajita Wrap

Ingredients:

- four large tortillas

- two boneless, skinless chicken breasts, grilled and sliced

- one red bell pepper, sliced

- one green bell pepper, sliced

- one onion, sliced

- half cupful shredded cheddar cheese

- Sour cream

- Salsa

Instructions:

1. Preheat your griddle to medium-high heat.

2. Grill the chicken breasts on the griddle until cooked through, then slice.

3. Sauté the sliced bell peppers and onions on the griddle until tender.

4. In each tortilla, layer chicken, sautéed peppers and onions, shredded cheddar cheese, sour cream, and salsa.

5. Wrap the tortillas and grill on the griddle for about two minutes per side, or until they are warm and slightly crispy.

Duration: Approximately eight minutes

Nutrients *(per wrap):*

- Caloric content: 400

- Amino content: 32g

- Carb content: 30g

- Fatty acid: 18g

10. Portobello Mushroom and Swiss Burger

Ingredients:

- four Portobello mushroom caps

- four hamburger buns

- four slices of Swiss cheese

- Olive oil

- Balsamic vinegar

- Salt and pepper to taste

Instructions:

1. Preheat your griddle to medium-high heat.

2. Brush the Portobello mushroom caps with olive oil and balsamic vinegar, then season with salt and pepper.

3. Grill the mushroom caps on the griddle for about four-five minutes per side, or until they are tender.

4. Place a slice of Swiss cheese on each mushroom cap and let it melt.

5. Toast the hamburger buns on the griddle.

6. Assemble the sandwiches with Portobello mushrooms and your choice of condiments.

Duration: Approximately ten minutes

Nutrients (per sandwich):

- Caloric content: 320

- Amino content: 15g

- Carb content: 35g

- Fatty acid: 14g

CHAPTER 13:
FLATBREADS AND PIZZA

1. Margherita Flatbread Pizza

Ingredients:

- one pre-made pizza dough or flatbread

- half cupful tomato sauce

- one half cupful fresh mozzarella cheese, sliced

- one cupful cherry tomatoes, sliced

- Fresh basil leaves

- Olive oil

- Salt and pepper to taste

Instructions:

1. Preheat your griddle to medium-high heat.

2. Roll out the pizza dough or place the flatbread on the griddle.

3. Spread a layer of tomato sauce over the dough or flatbread.

4. Arrange the mozzarella cheese and cherry tomato slices evenly.

5. Season with salt and pepper.

6. Grill the pizza on the griddle for about three-four minutes, or until the crust is crispy and the cheese is melted.

7. Garnish with fresh basil leaves and drizzle with olive oil.

Duration: Approximately five minutes

Nutrients (per portion):

- Caloric content: 320

- Amino content: 15g

- Carb content: 25g

- Fatty acid: 18g

2. BBQ Chicken Flatbread

Ingredients:

- one pre-made pizza dough or flatbread

- half cupful BBQ sauce

- one cupful cooked chicken breast, shredded

- half cupful red onion, thinly sliced

- one half cupful shredded cheddar cheese

- Fresh cilantro leaves

- Olive oil

Instructions:

1. Preheat your griddle to medium-high heat.

2. Roll out the pizza dough or place the flatbread on the griddle.

3. Spread a layer of BBQ sauce over the dough or flatbread.

4. Add shredded chicken, red onion, and shredded cheddar cheese evenly.

5. Grill the pizza on the griddle for about three-four minutes, or until the crust is crispy and the cheese is melted.

6. Garnish with fresh cilantro leaves and drizzle with olive oil.

Duration: Approximately five minutes

Nutrients (per portion):

- Caloric content: 350

- Amino content: 20g

- Carb content: 28g

- Fatty acid: 18g

3. Pesto and Sun-Dried Tomato Flatbread

Ingredients:

- one pre-made pizza dough or flatbread

- half cupful pesto sauce

- half cupful sun-dried tomatoes, sliced

- one cupful mozzarella cheese, shredded

- one-fourth cupful pine nuts

- Fresh basil leaves

- Olive oil

Instructions:

1. Preheat your griddle to medium-high heat.

2. Roll out the pizza dough or place the flatbread on the griddle.

3. Spread a layer of pesto sauce over the dough or flatbread.

4. Add sun-dried tomatoes, mozzarella cheese, and pine nuts evenly.

5. Grill the pizza on the griddle for about three-four minutes, or until the crust is crispy and the cheese is melted.

6. Garnish with fresh basil leaves and drizzle with olive oil.

Duration: Approximately five minutes

Nutrients *(per portion)*:

- Caloric content: 310

- Amino content: 10g

- Carb content: 20g

- Fatty acid: 22g

4. Greek Flatbread with Tzatziki

Ingredients:

- one pre-made pizza dough or flatbread

- half cupful Tzatziki sauce

- half cupful cucumber, diced

- half cupful cherry tomatoes, halved

- one-fourth cupful red onion, thinly sliced

- half cupful feta cheese, crumbled

- Kalamata olives, pitted and sliced

- Fresh dill, chopped

- Olive oil

- Salt and pepper to taste

Instructions:

1. Preheat your griddle to medium-high heat.

2. Roll out the pizza dough or place the flatbread on the griddle.

3. Spread a layer of Tzatziki sauce over the dough or flatbread.

4. Add cucumber, cherry tomatoes, red onion, feta cheese, and Kalamata olives evenly.

5. Season with salt, pepper, and fresh dill.

6. Grill the pizza on the griddle for about three-four minutes, or until the crust is crispy.

7. Drizzle with olive oil.

Duration: Approximately five minutes

Nutrients (per portion):

- Caloric content: 290

- Amino content: 10g

- Carb content: 25g

- Fatty acid: 17g

5. Breakfast Flatbread with Eggs and Bacon

Ingredients:

- one pre-made pizza dough or flatbread

- four large eggs

- four slices of bacon, cooked and crumbled

- half cupful cheddar cheese, shredded

- Fresh chives, chopped

- Salt and pepper to taste

Instructions:

1. Preheat your griddle to medium-high heat.

2. Roll out the pizza dough or place the flatbread on the griddle.

3. Make small wells in the dough or flatbread for the eggs.

4. Crack an egg into each well and sprinkle with salt and pepper.

5. Add crumbled bacon and cheddar cheese over the flatbread.

6. Grill the pizza on the griddle for about three-four minutes, or until the eggs are cooked to your desired level.

7. Garnish with fresh chives.

Duration: Approximately five minutes

Nutrients (per portion):

- Caloric content: 320

- Amino content: 17g

- Carb content: 20g

- Fatty acid: 20g

CHAPTER 14:
GRIDDLED PASTAS

1. Griddled Shrimp Scampi Pasta

Ingredients:

- one lb large shrimp, peeled and deveined

- eight oz linguine or spaghetti

- four cloves garlic, minced

- one-fourth cupful unsalted butter

- one-fourth cupful olive oil

- one-fourth cupful fresh lemon juice

- one-fourth cupful fresh parsley, chopped

- Red pepper flakes (optional)

- Salt and black pepper to taste

- Grated Parmesan cheese (for serving)

Instructions:

1. Preheat your griddle to medium-high heat.

2. Cook the pasta according to the package instructions until al dente.

3. In a large pan on the griddle, melt the butter and add the olive oil.

4. Add minced garlic and red pepper flakes (if using) and sauté for about one-two minutes.

5. Add the shrimp and cook for two-three minutes per side until they turn pink.

6. Stir in lemon juice, chopped parsley, and cooked pasta. Toss to combine.

7. Season with salt and black pepper.

8. Serve with grated Parmesan cheese.

Duration: Approximately 20 minutes

Nutrients (per portion):

- Caloric content: 420

- Amino content: 25g

- Carb content: 30g

- Fatty acid: 23g

2. Griddled Chicken Alfredo Pasta

Ingredients:

- two boneless, skinless chicken breasts

- eight oz fettuccine pasta

- two cupful heavy cream

- one cupful grated Parmesan cheese

- four cloves garlic, minced

- one-fourth cupful unsalted butter

- Salt and black pepper to taste

- Chopped fresh parsley (for garnish)

Instructions:

1. Preheat your griddle to medium-high heat.

2. Season the chicken breasts with salt and black pepper.

3. Grill the chicken on the griddle for about six-seven minutes per side until fully cooked.

4. Cook the fettuccine pasta according to the package instructions until al dente.

5. In a large pan on the griddle, melt the butter and add minced garlic. Sauté for one-two minutes.

6. Pour in heavy cream and grated Parmesan cheese. Stir until the sauce thickens.

7. Slice the grilled chicken and add it to the sauce.

8. Toss the cooked pasta in the Alfredo sauce.

9. Garnish with chopped fresh parsley.

Duration: Approximately Twenty Five minutes

Nutrients (per portion):

- Caloric content: 580

- Amino content: 30g

- Carb content: 40g

- Fatty acid: 35g

3. Griddled Pesto and Tomato Penne

Ingredients:

- 1two oz penne pasta

- half cupful pesto sauce

- two cupful cherry tomatoes, halved

- one-fourth cupful grated Parmesan cheese

- Fresh basil leaves (for garnish)

- Salt and black pepper to taste

Instructions:

1. Preheat your griddle to medium-high heat.

2. Cook the penne pasta according to the package instructions until al dente.

3. In a large bowl, mix the cooked pasta, pesto sauce, and cherry tomatoes.

4. Season with salt and black pepper.

5. Sprinkle with grated Parmesan cheese.

6. Garnish with fresh basil leaves.

Duration: Approximately fifteen minutes

Nutrients (per portion):

- Caloric content: 380

- Amino content: 12g

- Carb content: 45g

- Fatty acid: 18g

4. Griddled Spicy Sausage and Peppers Pasta

Ingredients:

- eight oz penne pasta

- one lb spicy Italian sausage, sliced

- one red bell pepper, sliced

- one yellow bell pepper, sliced

- half cupful marinara sauce

- one-fourth cupful grated Parmesan cheese

- Fresh basil leaves (for garnish)

- Salt and black pepper to taste

Instructions:

1. Preheat your griddle to medium-high heat.

2. Cook the penne pasta according to the package instructions until al dente.

3. In a large pan on the griddle, cook the sliced sausage until browned.

4. Add the sliced bell peppers and sauté until they are tender.

5. Stir in the marinara sauce and cooked pasta. Toss to combine.

6. Season with salt and black pepper.

7. Sprinkle with grated Parmesan cheese.

8. Garnish with fresh basil leaves.

Duration: Approximately 20 minutes

Nutrients (per portion):

- Caloric content: 480

- Amino content: 20g

- Carb content: 35g

- Fatty acid: 28g

5. Griddled Shrimp and Broccoli Alfredo

Ingredients:

- eight oz fettuccine pasta

- one lb large shrimp, peeled and deveined

- two cupful fresh broccoli florets

- one cupful Alfredo sauce

- one-fourth cupful grated Parmesan cheese

- four cloves garlic, minced

- two tablespoonful olive oil

- Salt and black pepper to taste

- Chopped fresh parsley (for garnish)

Instructions:

1. Preheat your griddle to medium-high heat.

2. Cook the fettuccine pasta according to the package instructions until al dente.

3. In a large pan on the griddle, heat the olive oil and add minced garlic. Sauté for one-two minutes.

4. Add shrimp and cook for two-three minutes per side until pink.

5. Add fresh broccoli florets and cook until tender.

6. Stir in Alfredo sauce and cooked pasta. Toss to combine.

7. Season with salt and black pepper.

8. Sprinkle with grated Parmesan cheese.

9. Garnish with chopped fresh parsley.

Duration: Approximately 20 minutes

Nutrients (per portion):

- Caloric content: 520

- Amino content: 30g

- Carb content: 35g

- Fatty acid: 28g

CHAPTER 15:
STIR-FRY NOODLES & FRIED RICE

1. Vegetable Stir-Fry Noodles

Ingredients:

- eight oz chow mein or lo mein noodles

- two tablespoonful sesame oil

- two cloves garlic, minced

- one cupful broccoli florets

- one cupful bell peppers, sliced

- one cupful carrots, julienned

- one cupful snow peas

- one-fourth cupful low-sodium soy sauce

- two tablespoonful oyster sauce

- one teaspoonful sugar

- one-fourth cupful green onions, chopped

- Sesame seeds (for garnish)

Instructions:

1. Cook the noodles according to the package instructions until al dente, then drain and set aside.

2. Preheat your griddle to medium-high heat.

3. In a large pan on the griddle, heat the sesame oil and sauté minced garlic for about one minute.

4. Add the broccoli, bell peppers, carrots, and snow peas. Stir-fry for about four-five minutes or until the vegetables are tender-crisp.

5. In a small bowl, whisk together soy sauce, oyster sauce, and sugar.

6. Add the cooked noodles to the pan and pour the sauce over them. Toss to combine and heat through.

7. Garnish with chopped green onions and sesame seeds.

Duration: Approximately fifteen minutes

Nutrients (per portion):

- Caloric content: 380

- Amino content: 8g

- Carb content: 60g

- Fatty acid: 12g

2. Chicken Fried Rice

Ingredients:

- two cupful cooked and chilled white rice

- one cupful cooked chicken breast, diced

- one cupful frozen mixed vegetables

- two eggs, beaten

- two tablespoonful vegetable oil

- two tablespoonful soy sauce

- half teaspoonful garlic powder

- half teaspoonful ginger

- Salt and pepper to taste

- Chopped green onions (for garnish)

Instructions:

1. Preheat your griddle to medium-high heat.

2. In a large pan on the griddle, heat vegetable oil.

3. Add the beaten eggs and scramble them until they're cooked but still moist. Remove from the pan and set aside.

4. In the same pan, add cooked chicken and frozen mixed vegetables. Stir-fry for about three-four minutes or until heated through.

5. Add cooked rice, soy sauce, garlic powder, ginger, and the scrambled eggs. Toss to combine.

6. Season with salt and pepper.

7. Garnish with chopped green onions.

Duration: Approximately fifteen minutes

Nutrients (per portion):

- Caloric content: 380

- Amino content: 20g

- Carb content: 45g

- Fatty acid: 14g

3. Beef and Broccoli Stir-Fry

Ingredients:

- one lb flank steak, sliced into thin strips

- two tablespoonful vegetable oil

- two cupful broccoli florets

- one-fourth cupful low-sodium soy sauce

- two tablespoonful oyster sauce

- two tablespoonful brown sugar

- two cloves garlic, minced

- one teaspoonful ginger

- two teaspoonful cornstarch

- Sesame seeds (for garnish)

- Cooked white or brown rice (for serving)

Instructions:

1. Preheat your griddle to medium-high heat.

2. In a large pan on the griddle, heat one tablespoon of vegetable oil.

3. Add sliced flank steak and stir-fry for about three-four minutes until browned. Remove from the pan and set aside.

4. In the same pan, add the remaining one tablespoon of vegetable oil and sauté minced garlic for about one minute.

5. Add broccoli florets and cook for four-five minutes or until tender.

6. In a small bowl, whisk together soy sauce, oyster sauce, brown sugar, ginger, and cornstarch.

7. Return the cooked beef to the pan, pour the sauce over it, and toss to combine. Cook for an additional two-three minutes until the sauce thickens.

8. Garnish with sesame seeds and serve over cooked rice.

Duration: Approximately 20 minutes

Nutrients (per portion, *without rice):*

- Caloric content: 300

- Amino content: 25g

- Carb content: 15g

- Fatty acid: 16g

4. Shrimp Pad Thai

Ingredients:

- eight oz rice noodles

- half lb large shrimp, peeled and deveined

- two cloves garlic, minced

- one-fourth cupful unsalted peanuts, chopped

- two eggs, beaten

- two tablespoonful vegetable oil

- three tablespoonful fish sauce

- one tablespoonful tamarind paste

- one tablespoonful sugar

- one cupful bean sprouts

- one-fourth cupful fresh cilantro, chopped

- Lime wedges (for garnish)

Instructions:

1. Cook the rice noodles according to the package instructions until al dente, then drain and set aside.

2. Preheat your griddle to medium-high heat.

3. In a large pan on the griddle, heat vegetable oil.

4. Add minced garlic and sauté for about one minute.

5. Add beaten eggs and scramble until they're cooked but still moist. Remove from the pan and set aside.

6. In the same pan, add shrimp and cook for two-three minutes per side until pink.

7. In a small bowl, whisk together fish sauce, tamarind paste, and sugar.

8. Add the cooked noodles, scrambled eggs, and sauce to the pan. Toss to combine.

9. Add bean sprouts and fresh cilantro.

10. Garnish with chopped peanuts and serve with lime wedges.

Duration: Approximately fifteen minutes

Nutrients (per portion):

- Caloric content: 380

- Amino content: 18g

- Carb content: 45g

- Fatty acid: 14g

5. Veggie and Tofu Stir-Fry Noodles

Ingredients:

- eight oz udon or soba noodles

- half block of firm tofu, cubed

- one cupful broccoli florets

- one cupful snap peas

- one cupful bell peppers, sliced

- two cloves garlic, minced

- one-fourth cupful low-sodium soy sauce

- two tablespoonful hoisin sauce

- one tablespoonful sesame oil

- one teaspoonful brown sugar

- one-fourth cupful green onions, chopped

- Sesame seeds (for garnish)

Instructions:

1. Cook the udon or soba noodles according to the package instructions until al dente, then drain and set aside.

2. Preheat your griddle to medium-high heat.

3. In a large pan on the griddle, heat sesame oil.

4. Add cubed tofu and stir-fry for about three-four minutes until browned. Remove from the pan and set aside.

5. In the same pan, add minced garlic and sauté for about one minute.

6. Add broccoli florets, snap peas, and bell peppers. Stir-fry for about four-five minutes or until the vegetables are tender-crisp.

7. In a small bowl, whisk together soy sauce, hoisin sauce, and brown sugar.

8. Return the tofu to the pan, pour the sauce over it, and toss to combine.

9. Add the cooked noodles and toss to coat.

10. Garnish with chopped green onions and sesame seeds.

Duration: Approximately 20 minutes

Nutrients (per portion):

- Caloric content: 380

- Amino content: 18g

- Carb content: 45g

- Fatty acid: 14g

CHAPTER 16:
DESSERT

1. Griddled Banana Foster

Ingredients:

- four ripe bananas, peeled and sliced

- one-fourth cupful unsalted butter

- half cupful brown sugar

- one-fourth cupful dark rum

- half teaspoonful ground cinnamon

- Vanilla ice cream

Instructions:

1. Preheat your griddle to medium-high heat.

2. In a large pan on the griddle, melt the butter and add brown sugar and ground cinnamon. Stir until sugar is dissolved.

3. Add the banana slices and sauté for two-three minutes until they are caramelized.

4. Carefully add the rum and let it flame (flambé) by tilting the pan toward the flame source or using a long lighter.

5. Let the flame subside and serve the bananas over a scoop of vanilla ice cream.

Duration: Approximately ten minutes

Nutrients (*per portion*, *without ice cream*):

- Caloric content: 180

- Amino content: 1g

- Carb content: 25g

- Fatty acid: 7g

2. Griddled Apple Cinnamon Pancakes

Ingredients:

- one cupful pancake mix

- 2/three cupful milk

- one egg

- one teaspoonful ground cinnamon

- one apple, peeled and diced

- two tablespoonful unsalted butter

- Maple syrup

Instructions:

1. Preheat your griddle to medium-high heat.

2. In a bowl, whisk together pancake mix, milk, egg, and ground cinnamon until smooth.

3. Melt one tablespoon of butter on the griddle and add diced apples. Sauté for about three minutes or until they're slightly tender.

4. Pour pancake batter over the apples to form pancakes.

5. Cook the pancakes for two-three minutes per side until they're golden brown.

6. Serve with maple syrup.

Duration: Approximately fifteen minutes

Nutrients (per portion, without syrup):

- Caloric content: 250

- Amino content: 6g

- Carb content: 35g

- Fatty acid: 9g

3. Griddled S'mores Quesadillas

Ingredients:

- four large flour tortillas

- one cupful milk chocolate chips

- one cupful mini marshmallows

- half cupful graham cracker crumbs

- two tablespoonful unsalted butter

- Chocolate sauce (optional)

Instructions:

1. Preheat your griddle to medium-high heat.

2. Place one tortilla on the griddle and sprinkle half with chocolate chips, marshmallows, and graham cracker crumbs.

3. Fold the other half of the tortilla over to form a half-moon.

4. Spread a thin layer of butter on the top of the quesadilla.

5. Grill for about two-three minutes per side or until it's golden and the chocolate and marshmallows are melted.

6. Repeat with the remaining tortillas.

7. Drizzle with chocolate sauce if desired.

Duration: Approximately ten minutes

Nutrients *(per quesadilla):*

- Caloric content: 400

- Amino content: 5g

- Carb content: 60g

- Fatty acid: 16g

4. Griddled Pineapple with Vanilla Ice Cream

Ingredients:

- one pineapple, peeled, cored, and sliced into rings

- two tablespoonful brown sugar

- one teaspoonful ground cinnamon

- Vanilla ice cream

- Caramel sauce (optional)

Instructions:

1. Preheat your griddle to medium-high heat.

2. In a bowl, mix brown sugar and ground cinnamon.

3. Sprinkle the sugar mixture over the pineapple rings.

4. Grill the pineapple on the griddle for about two-three minutes per side until it's caramelized.

5. Serve the grilled pineapple with a scoop of vanilla ice cream.

6. Drizzle with caramel sauce if desired.

Duration: Approximately ten minutes

*Nutrients (**per portion**, without caramel sauce):*

- Caloric content: 180

- Amino content: 1g

- Carb content: 45g

- Fatty acid: 1g

5. Griddled Strawberry Shortcake

Ingredients:

- one lb fresh strawberries, hulled and sliced

- one-fourth cupful granulated sugar

- one cupful heavy cream

- two tablespoonful powdered sugar

- one teaspoonful vanilla extract

- four store-bought shortcakes

- Fresh mint leaves (for garnish)

Instructions:

1. In a bowl, combine sliced strawberries and granulated sugar. Let them sit for about ten minutes to macerate.

2. Preheat your griddle to medium-high heat.

3. In a mixing bowl, whip heavy cream, powdered sugar, and vanilla extract until stiff peaks form.

4. Split the shortcakes in half and grill the cut sides on the griddle for about one-two minutes until they're lightly toasted.

5. To assemble, place a grilled shortcake half on a plate, top with macerated strawberries, a dollop of whipped cream, and another shortcake half. Repeat for each shortcake.

6. Garnish with fresh mint leaves.

Duration: Approximately ten minutes

Nutrients (per portion):

- Caloric content: 300

- Amino content: 2g

- Carb content: 45g

- Fatty acid: 15g

FAQS

Here are answers to some common FAQs about using and maintaining a Blackstone griddle:

Griddle vs. Grill: Q: What's the difference between a griddle and a grill? A: Griddles and grills serve different purposes. Griddles have a flat cooking surface ideal for cooking items like pancakes, stir-fry, and sandwiches. Grills have open grates for grilling meats and imparting smoky flavors. While grills are perfect for steaks, burgers, and kebabs, griddles are great for breakfast foods, vegetables, and more.

Dealing with Rust: Q: My Blackstone griddle has rust spots. What should I do? A: To remove rust, scrub the affected areas with steel wool or a wire brush until the rust is gone. Afterward, re-season your griddle with a thin layer of cooking oil to prevent further rusting. Regular maintenance and keeping your griddle covered when not in use can help prevent rust.

Cast Iron Griddles: Q: Are Blackstone griddles made of cast iron? A: Yes, most Blackstone griddles have a cast iron cooking surface. Cast iron provides excellent heat retention and even cooking, making it a popular choice for griddles.

Dishwasher-Safe Tools: Q: Can I put my Blackstone griddle tools in the dishwasher? A: It's generally not recommended to put griddle tools in the dishwasher as the high heat and moisture can cause them to rust or deteriorate faster. Hand wash them with warm, soapy water, and dry thoroughly to maintain their longevity.

Cleaning and Re-seasoning: Q: How should I clean and re-season my Blackstone griddle? A: After each use, scrape off any food residue with a griddle scraper while the griddle is still warm. For a deeper clean, use a mixture of water and mild dish soap. Rinse, dry, and then apply a thin layer of cooking oil while the griddle is warm to re-season it. This will help maintain a non-stick surface and prevent rust.

Preventing Scratches: Q: What can I do to prevent scratches on my griddle surface? A: Avoid using metal utensils that can scratch the griddle. Instead, opt for tools made of wood, silicone, or heat-resistant plastic. These utensils are less likely to damage the cooking surface.

Handling Plate Deformities: Q: What should I do if my griddle plate becomes deformed? A: If your griddle plate becomes deformed, check if it's still under warranty. In some cases, the manufacturer may offer replacements. To avoid plate deformities, always store your griddle on a level surface and protect it from heavy objects that could press on the plate.

Remember, proper care and maintenance are essential to extend the life of your Blackstone griddle and ensure it continues to deliver delicious meals.

CONCLUSION

In the journey through the "Blackstone Griddle Bible," we've unlocked the secrets of grilling mastery on a Blackstone griddle. It has been a flavorful exploration of not just recipes, but a culinary philosophy that elevates outdoor cooking to an art form.

From the very beginning, our dedication to family and the love of good food set the stage for a memorable culinary experience. We've delved into the basics, from choosing the right Blackstone griddle to understanding the differences between cast iron and stainless steel. We've explored the essential equipment and learned how to care for our griddle, ensuring it serves us well for years to come.

The world of griddle cooking opened up as we discovered various techniques, from frying to wood pellet griddling, both easy and advanced. We explored the best cuts of meat and their ideal grill temperatures, providing a roadmap to delicious, perfectly cooked meals.

The "Blackstone Griddle Bible" is not just about technique; it's a treasure trove of tips, tricks, and a guide to using sauces and seasonings effectively. And as stewards of the environment, we've embraced eco-friendly griddling practices, promoting sustainability and responsibility in our culinary pursuits.

The heart of this book, the recipes, have been carefully crafted to delight your taste buds. From sizzling breakfasts to Tex-Mex feasts, succulent burgers to fresh fish, hearty sandwiches to delectable desserts, and even griddled pizzas and stir-fry noodles, we've left no culinary stone unturned.

But it's not just about the recipes; it's about the joy of griddling, the thrill of sizzling perfection, and the satisfaction of sharing delightful meals with family and friends. The "Blackstone Griddle Bible" is an invitation to turn every backyard barbecue into a gourmet feast, making you the undisputed grill master of your neighborhood.

As you embark on your griddling adventures, remember that the true essence of grilling is not just in the food; it's in the memories created, the laughter shared, and the connections strengthened around your Blackstone griddle. It's a journey that transcends the ordinary and transforms every meal into a celebration.

Thank you for joining us on this savory expedition. May your griddle always be hot, your ingredients forever fresh, and your meals infused with the passion that this "Blackstone Griddle Bible" has ignited. Happy griddling, and may your culinary horizons be limitless!

BONUS:

TUTORIAL ON CONVERTING BLACKSTONE TO NATURAL GAS

DOWNLOAD NOW YOUR BONUS

Made in the USA
Columbia, SC
17 December 2023

28861010R00072